WHERE DOES ALL THE MONEY GO?

- The Department of Education doesn't teach a single one of our children—and only contributes 6% of the massive cost of education.

- The Department of Transportation covers less than half the cost of our roads and highways—and that comes out of the gas tax fund, not the Treasury.

- The Department of Energy doesn't pay our electricity, gas, or oil bills, and provides cheap energy to only a handful of Americans.

- The Department of Health and Human Services doesn't furnish the great majority of Americans with *any* medical care.

- The Department of Agriculture provides services mainly to farmers, whose number *decreases* every year, even as the number of Department of Agriculture bureaucrats *increases*.

So what happens to our tax dollars?

Read The Government Racket—the book that uncovers the hundreds of ways Washington is bankrupting our country.

THE GOVERNMENT RACKET

Washington Waste from A to Z

Martin L. Gross

BANTAM BOOKS
New York · Toronto · London · Sydney · Auckland

THE GOVERNMENT RACKET
A Bantam Book / July 1992

ISBN 0-553-37175-4

Published simultaneously in the United States and Canada

Bantam Books are published by Bantam Books, a division of
Bantam Doubleday Dell Publishing Group, Inc. Its trade-
mark, consisting of the words "Bantam Books" and the por-
trayal of a rooster, is Registered in U.S. Patent and Trademark
Office and in other countries. Marca Registrada, Bantam
Books, 666 Fifth Avenue, New York, New York 10103.

PRINTED IN THE UNITED STATES OF AMERICA

FFG   0

To Thomas Jefferson,
From whom all liberty springs

ACKNOWLEDGMENTS

THE FOLLOWING ORGANIZATIONS and individuals have been extremely helpful in the work of researching this volume:

Office of the Clerk of the House of Representatives; Office of the Secretary of the Senate; Media Affairs department of the White House; Office of the Vice President; Historians of the Department of Agriculture; Public affairs section and auditors of the General Accounting Office; the Congressional Budget Office; the Office of Management and Budget; the Office of Personnel Management; Public Affairs sections of the Departments of Commerce, Labor, Education, Agriculture, Transportation, Health and Human Services; the Legislative Appropriations Subcommittee of the House of Representatives; the Senate Judiciary Committee; Public Affairs sections of the Air Force and the Department of Defense.

Also, the Citizens Against Government Waste; the National Taxpayers Union; Citizens for a Sound Economy; the Senate Rules Committee; the offices of the Majority and Minority Leaders of the House; the Speaker's Office; the House Finance Office; the Federal Election Commission; the Rural Electrification Administration; the Government Printing Office; the National Furniture Center; the Federal Highway Administration; the U.S. Postal

ACKNOWLEDGMENTS

Service; the Small Business Administration; the Bureau of Reclamation; the Bureau of Indian Affairs; and various individual Congressmen and their aides.

As well as the Harry S Truman Library in Independence, Missouri; the John F. Kennedy Library in Boston, Massachusetts; the National Archives; the General Services Administration; the U.S. Forest Service; the Interior Department; the Social Security Administration; the Western Area Power Administration; the Capitol Architect's Office; and many other government agencies and the more than one hundred officials who gave freely of their time.

Without them, this critique of the federal government could not have been written.

I would also like to thank my editor, Barbara Alpert, my publisher, Matthew Shear, and my agent, John Hawkins.

CONTENTS

CONTENTS

CONTENTS

CONTENTS

CONTENTS

CONTENTS

THE GOVERNMENT RACKET

PROLOGUE

Behind the Government Racket

THERE IS DISQUIET in the land.

For the first time in decades, the majority of Americans are seriously debating the integrity and judgment of their federal government. Not that they are fully armed with information—they are not—but there is a gnawing concern, an undercurrent of grumbling overheard on supermarket checkout lines and voiced in public-opinion polls.

"Why does Uncle Sam spend so much money?" people ask. And unspoken is the obvious question: "Why don't *I* seem to be sharing in the rewards of my own government?"

There's little doubt that the American public is confused and frustrated by what's happening in Washington. Every few months, a supposed debate about "government waste" erupts in the capital and infuriates the nation.

There is either a rash of bounced checks, or a campaign contribution scandal, or a fight about spending $500,000 to construct a memorial to Lawrence Welk. Or, the President of the United States gets angry at Congress for wasting the nation's money on pet "pork barrel" projects.

The Republicans point an accusing finger at the Democrats who control the Hill. The Democrats respond that the last two Republican presidents have more than

1

doubled the federal deficit. It becomes a partisan brouhaha with great pulses of heat, but no illumination.

The people seem smarter than the politicians. They suspect that something even messier than "pork" is involved, and they're asking the right questions:

"Is the government truly my friend? Or if not my enemy, is the government indifferent to my concerns? Is the current $1.5 trillion budget, almost 25% of which is borrowed, and which is supported by record-high taxes, necessary? Is the money being legitimately spent or is it being squandered by bureaucrats and politicians instead of benefiting the American people?"

Americans are asking these penetrating questions regardless of party or ideology, and not always in the nicest of tones. A consensus of disappointment with Washington that transcends partisanship is developing, making for a confrontation of "them" versus "us."

People are suspicious that something is *fundamentally* wrong in Washington. And they are right. Hundreds of billions of dollars are being taken from them each year under false pretenses. In fact, waste of enormous proportions is built into the federal system, though most of it is expertly hidden. Waste is more prevalent than efficiency; more common than good works. If it continues at its present pace, not only will it bankrupt the nation fiscally, it will destroy us morally as well.

Thus the reason for this book. *The Government Racket* will show, in 75 different areas, how deeply incompetence and misdirection infect the root of the American government and cripple its ability to serve all its citizens.

Unfortunately, few people understand how Washington really works. The reported scandals are mere blemishes on the national skin, eruptions that don't truly reveal the erosion going on within the body politic. If the public were to know the full story, they would probably conclude that their federal government is an expensive, arcane, often irrational, self-serving, self-perpetuating operation that has to be radically reformed.

One reason for people's frustration is that they feel detached from Washington—that most of what goes on is not directly connected to their own lives. And their suspicions are correct.

We can relate to local, even state government, which provide tangible services, from garbage collection to police protection. But what does the federal government—which takes the lion's share of our tax money—actually do for us?

We're all aware of the national involvement in defense and foreign affairs. But how does the government affect the life of the average American at home?

What is generally not taken into account is the Tenth Amendment to the Constitution, the last item in the Bill of Rights. It leaves to the states and the people all powers not specifically granted to the federal government, which are very few in number. To circumvent that amendment, Washington has developed thousands of projects on which it spends trillions, but for which it is seldom held accountable.

The result is a strange system—one that exists nowhere else in the developed democratic world—in which Washington collects our money, but provides few direct services.

The Department of Education doesn't teach a single one of our children. That's a local function, to which Washington contributes only 6% of the cost. Our roads and highways are mainly paid for by states and municipalities. Since few of us are farmers, we're ineligible for the bounty of the Department of Agriculture.

The Department of Energy doesn't pay our utility bills and provides cheap power for only a relative handful of Americans. The Department of Health and Human Services doesn't furnish the great majority of Americans with medical care. And if we're senior citizens, our benefit checks are being diluted every day by the government's wanton use of the money paid it for the aged.

There's no doubt that some of the frustration stems from the exaggerated promises of government, which we have naively accepted. Listening to politicians over the last two decades, during which the federal budget has grown an average of 10% per year no matter which party controlled the Congress or the White House, one would expect that a golden deliverance was about to come from Washington.

But people are becoming more sophisticated and beginning to realize that big government doesn't necessarily mean beneficent or responsive government. After decades of time and trillions of dollars, government loses its claim to legitimacy when it fails to fulfill its obligations. The nation begins to doubt, as it now has, that the promises were made in good faith. Government is then seen as a failure, a fallacy, a myth, a racket.

In some ways, in fact, our federal establishment—which bears little resemblance to the one set up by the Founding Fathers—might be compared to a numbers racket. If you're lucky, you'll beat the odds and get a payoff. If not, all you're left with is a stub.

If family income is low, for instance, a youngster can qualify for a generous federal Pell Grant to pay for college. But if the family earns more than the cut-off ceiling, bank loans are all they can look forward to. If you retire at age sixty-two on Social Security, you've hit an actuarial jackpot, receiving much more in benefits than you've put in. But if you continue working at a medium wage, until you're seventy, you collect nothing from Uncle Sam and keep paying into the Social Security fund. As long as you work, no matter how old you are, you keep paying.

If you're a farmer, even a wealthy one, you can get crop subsidies and low-interest federal loans. If you're a businessman, you may be one of the lucky few (including doctors) who receive a government-guaranteed loan from the Small Business Administration. If not, you suffer the vagaries of the uncertain marketplace.

If you're poor, Washington provides food stamps, Aid to Families with Dependent Children payments, and subsidized housing. If you're rich, you can buy tax-free municipal bonds and thumb your nose at the IRS. But if you're a working stiff, you can expect only anxiety and the government's hand deep in your pocket.

Now, more than at any time in American history, the government seems determined to help selected people, not the nation as a whole. That wasn't the case after World War II, when without any means test, 14 million veterans and their families benefited immensely from Harry Truman's GI Bill of Rights. And so did the rest of the country.

Today's frustration with the federal government increases as the tax burden rises. The reality of the $1.5 trillion budget becomes more concrete when Americans realize they will have to work until almost the middle of May to pay off Washington and other governments before they can take home a penny for themselves. Sometimes it seems there's not enough money left over for the *real* nation to operate on.

Much of government spending is dictated by the needs of special-interest groups—banks, lawyers, doctors and hospitals, corporations, farmers, universities, real-estate people, researchers, unions, ranchers, utilities, foreign interests, scientists, insurance companies, defense contractors, foundations, oil and gas firms. Anyone you can think of—except the working middle class who pay the bulk of our taxes.

The most powerful special-interest group is the wasteful, inefficient federal government itself. The best comparison might be to a charity that collects a fortune in contributions, but keeps too much of it to run its own operation, then dispenses the rest without rhyme or reason.

If America is wedded to capitalism (as the former USSR was to socialism), then the federal government has invented a system of its own: *bureaucratism*. It flourishes in the secure, affluent Beltway area around Washington, one which experiences no recessions and lives off the sacrifices of the rest of the nation. It supports a class of privileged people, who, whatever their ideology, are united in one cause—taking in, then spending, our tax money, often recklessly.

That's the core reason for this book. Through investigative reporting, research and analysis, study of the budget document, and interviews with scores of agency officials, the federal government will be dissected—in a nonpartisan manner—to show that waste is not just a scandalous exception, but has become indigenous to the Washington Establishment, that informal union of bureaucrats and elected politicians who run the country.

We're often reminded of the old days of "big government" when FDR presided over a nation in a deep depression. Surprisingly, it was all done with a small bureaucracy and rather cheaply. In 1938, the federal government handled welfare, WPA (Works Progress Administration), and programs too numerous to mention, with an income of only 7.7% of the Gross National Product.

Today, with supposedly "modern" government, loaded down with computers, complex theories, and a large cadre of educated personnel, federal expenditures are at an all-time high—25% of the total national product in 1991 with a $400 billion deficit in 1992 to boot. Promises to eliminate that deficit have all proven hollow. People are beginning to fear that, like slick home-siding salesmen, our politicians *know* that they can't possibly deliver on their claims.

Many economists even believe that Washington is a root cause of America's unstable economy—that its $4 trillion debt creates the high long-term interest and home-mortgage rates that hold back our growth.

Why has this happened?

In this book, we will try to reveal the false concepts, bad management, and empty promises that shape today's federal government. By reporting on the key segments of the Washington Establishment, arranged alphabetically in relatively short units, we will offer numerous examples of the workings of a federal city—and thus a nation— gone fiscally mad.

Abraham Lincoln, in speaking to a caller at the White House during the Civil War, remarked that "you can't fool all the people all the time." The federal government attempts to refute Old Abe's maxim, but this author is hopeful that by the time readers have finished this book, they will be expert enough on how our money is being squandered to restore Lincoln's status as a seer.

If the reader will indulge me, I'd like to peek ahead just a bit. The last alphabetical item in this book is ZOOS. The United States operates two in the nation's capital. One is in Rock Creek Park. The other is the federal government.

And now, on to Washington.

1

AGRICULTURE, DEPARTMENT OF

Cornucopia of Waste

SOME 30 YEARS AGO, the famed British satirist C. North-cote Parkinson came up with Parkinson's Law, a formula that describes the strange behavior of government bureaucracies. As the British Navy demobilized after World War I, for example, the Admiralty staff rose in inverse ratio. That is, the fewer the ships, the more the bureaucrats.

Parkinson's Law has come to life in the American government, especially in the Department of Agriculture, where farms have replaced ships in his prophetic equation. At the turn of the century, the Department had 3000 employees to handle 5 million farms, what were to become the breadbasket of the world. By 1935, there were 6.3 million American farmers and the D of A had 20,000 employees.

Today, Parkinson's Law is in full swing in Washington. The number of farmers has dropped precipitously to 2.1 million, half of whom are part-timers. Meanwhile, the number of government farm employees (excluding Food Stamp and Forest Service personnel) has grown to 60,000. As farms have *dropped* to one-third in number in the last half century, federal farm bureaucrats have taken up the slack, *increasing* threefold.

If we plot the figures on a graph, the future is statistically frightening.

By the year 2040, the number of full-time American farmers will be down to 150,000, while the number of D of A workers will have reached that same level. Surely, we Americans will have achieved the ultimate victory of bureaucracy—one federal employee figuratively kibitzing each farmer as he plows his rows.

The number of farmers continues to decrease each year, but not surprisingly, the money spent surveying and recording their activities keeps rising, another case of Parkinson's Law at work. The Department's National Agricultural Service and its sister agency, the Economic Research Service, together employ more than 2000 people. Not only does that cost the taxpayers $150 million a year, but their budgets have gone up 25% just since 1990 as the farms they count continue to disappear.

The Department of Agriculture, whose excess has been shaped by farm-region politicians making sweetheart deals with their city brethren, is a cornucopia of waste without peer. It now costs the taxpayers $56 billion a year as it stubbornly maintains outdated, expensive farm programs.

"Our farm programs helped the part-time farmers who had outside jobs by giving them subsidies," says a government official charged with overseeing the farm programs. "It also helped the big farmers to make more money. It's cost the government a fortune, but overall, it didn't help the little 'family farmer' it was designed for."

(See FARMERS, LOANS; FARMERS, SUBSIDIES; MILK; WOOL AND MOHAIR; HONEY; even URBAN GARDENS.)

What is the solution? Simple. Cut the legions of farm watchers in half immediately. Surprisingly, the efficient American farm economy will prosper and the taxpayers' savings will be in the double-digit billions.

Even Mr. Parkinson will be pleased.

2

AIRCRAFT, GOVERNMENT

The High-Status Skies

THE UNITED STATES GOVERNMENT owns and operates 1200 airplanes, with pilots, airfields, mechanics, and all that's needed to keep them aloft.

So? Every country needs an air force to protect itself, doesn't it? Since when are military aircraft a novelty?

But these are not military planes. These are *civilian* aircraft of 100 different varieties owned and operated by *civilian* government agencies like the Departments of Energy and Transportation. Their purpose? Mainly to fly their executives and employees around the country without their having to suffer the inconvenience of mixing with the sweaty taxpaying public.

Piloted private planes have become an exalted status symbol among Washington bureaucrats. They're also a great waste of money. Even usually understated government auditors are aghast: "Federal ownership of planes is inefficient and wasteful," says a General Accounting Office report.

But typically, nothing has been done to halt this near-secret boondoggle. Bureaucrats continue to slide Cessnas and Gulfstreams into their budgets by falsely claiming that the plane is needed for a technical "mission."

Say the auditors: "Some agencies classify certain

aircraft as mission-related even though the aircraft are used primarily to provide transportation or to keep their pilots qualified."

In reality, federal executives use the aircraft not only to fly themselves and employees on business, but to transport their parties to convention resorts and other desirable destinations.

Checking on two Department of Transportation planes, the auditors found that their use for routine transportation was not justified: commercial travel would have been cheaper; flights were made with only a few passengers on board; and the planes were used to fly high-ranking bureaucrats and Coast Guard officials—often with their spouses and guests—on trips in the U.S. and even overseas.

Can this misuse of taxpayer money be halted? First, that requires that someone actually be in charge of the government, which as we shall see (CHIEF EXECUTIVE) is not the case. In Washington, everyone fends, and plots, for himself. For example, when the Inspector General of the Department of Energy advised the Bonneville Power Authority that buying a new aircraft would violate government guidelines, the BPA went ahead and bought the plane anyway.

How expensive is this craving for the bureaucrat's ultimate status symbol?

Very. The cost of the aircraft has been estimated at $2 billion. The depreciation runs at least $200 million a year. The annual upkeep costs another $800 million. There's also the added cost of civilian airports and military bases that accommodate the planes. And if that's not enough, government agencies *lease* still another 5000 private planes each year at a cost of $100 million.

Because the planes are not standardized, each different

model—from over 25 different manufacturers—requires its own specially trained pilot, mechanics, and individual spare parts, raising the cost even further.

The tariff runs the taxpayer well over a billion dollars a year, a figure that will grow considerably as the old planes are replaced by new ones.

The solution:

Sell off most of the aircraft and put the proceeds into the Treasury. We'll also save the billion dollars in annual upkeep.

And as the late Senator Everett McKinley Dirksen of Illinois used to remind us: "A billion here and a billion there, and soon you're talking about real money."

3

AIRLINES, GOVERNMENT

Coffee, Tea, or Freebie?

WHEN JOHN SUNUNU, President Bush's former Chief of Staff, jumped on and off government Boeing 707s and Gulfstream jets at Andrews Air Force Base on personal trips, he set off a scandal that cost him his job. Secretary of State James Baker admitted to taking pleasure flights on government planes, but he reimbursed the Treasury and stayed on the team.

Fine. But the real scandal is the government airline itself—the 89th Airlift Wing, which is a politician-bureaucrat's dream. People are surprised to learn that the government owns an airline, as well they should be. Especially since the 89th is the most inefficient, wasteful, and expensive one in the nation.

Based eleven miles from Washington, it transports government bureaucrats, Congressmen, Senators, military brass—from Cabinet people and Army Generals down to lowly staffers on House Committees—all over the country and the world, free of charge. It is, as the 89th advertises itself, "The airline of the VIPs."

The notion of traveling on a government plane conjures up images of jump seats on a rusty cargo plane. But that's old World War II stuff. The President's two 747 flying palaces, which cost taxpayers $410 million, are the most elegant large planes in the world. But the other 23 passenger planes in the 89th fleet, which include Boeing 707s, DC-9s, and Gulfstream III jets, are almost as comfy—much like commercial airliners, except in their cost to the taxpayers.

Do we really need the 89th? The President, Vice President, Secretaries of State and Defense, and the Chairman of the Joint Chiefs, plus foreign dignitaries, need access to such planes. But for the others, it's merely a perk, a status symbol that says they don't have to rub elbows with the hoi polloi on regular airliners.

The price to taxpayers is enormous.

Let's look at the numbers. The 89th has 6000 employees taking care of the 25 planes plus 19 helicopters, an outrageous person-to-plane ratio. According to figures supplied by an Air Force official, the 89th is the least busy airline in the world. Aside from the helicopters, the planes make only 800 flights a year, which means the typical airliner spends most of its time on the ground, burning more money than gasoline.

The government refuses to release figures on how many passengers they fly a year, but one Air Force spokesman estimated a total of 10,000. That means that most planes take off near-empty.

With payroll and benefits for employees, in addition to the operating budget, the cost of the planes, and depreciation, the 89th—without the Air Force Ones—runs the taxpayers over a half billion dollars a year, or almost a half million dollars a flight, at least *twenty* times more than the cost of flying on commercial planes. Even if the number of passengers is actually twice their estimate, or 20,000, the typical traveler costs the U.S. taxpayer about $25,000 a flight.

As a comparison, let's take Southwest Airline, a plucky

little company out of Texas, which has 10,000 employees for 124 planes and turns a profit every year. Southwest makes over a thousand flights *a day*—not a year—and carried 22 million passengers in 1991.

My suggestion? Keep five planes in the 89th for the care of the Super VIPs. Sell the others and contract with Southwest to run the Andrews passenger business, then return the cash to the Treasury.

Or better still, close down most of the 89th.

The United States also operates a second airline, the 375th Airlift Wing out of Scott AFB in Illinois. The 375th has 77 small jets—Lears, Beechcrafts, and Gulfstreams—and does have a very legitimate mission. Last year, it successfully flew more than 70,000 servicemen on medical flights.

But the other half of their mission is like the 89th's, if for less-exalted passengers. The 375th has facilities at twelve Air Force bases, from California to Maryland, and in addition to flying military people, politicians, and bureaucrats around the country, it takes almost everyone—except regular taxpayers—on a free "space available" basis, which is almost always. That includes traveling for personal reasons, even going on vacation.

The free passenger list, says the Military Air Command, covers service personnel; reservists in the armed forces holding down civilian jobs; retired members of the services, also working elsewhere; and the families of all of the above.

Where can they fly? Almost anywhere in the States on the 375th, then connect with MAC's large planes for free overseas travel to Scotland, Italy, Germany, Peru, Turkey, Iceland, Greenland, Norway, Puerto Rico, Spain,

Guam, Japan, Singapore, Hawaii, Panama, Azores, South Korea, Philippines, Greece, Israel, Argentina, Bahamas, Bolivia, Indonesia, Thailand, Venezuela, and Australia.

Is this minor air traffic? Hardly.

Last year, over a half million people used these freebies for personal reasons, costing Uncle Sam at least $100 million.

The only catch? The government demands a $10 fee.

4

BUDGET, FEDERAL

Anyone for ZBB?

THE FISCAL 1993 FEDERAL BUDGET is a hefty eight-pound document of sheer wonder, uncommon confusion, and massive irrationality.

The $43 monster (available at any government bookstore) was created like all its predecessors, in a manner calculated to keep the budget high and the deficit soaring. The federal budget has grown an average of 10% a year for the past two decades, the core reason for the $4 trillion national debt.

The 2000-page document, with its 190,000 entries and 4000-subject index, can stymie the most energetic of critics, which, of course, was one motive of its creators. (This writer admits to having read or scanned every one of its pages, a boast not even the President or the Speaker of the House can make.)

The 1993 budget was set in late 1991, at the height of the recession, when the GNP wasn't growing at all. Yet it called for $1.515 *trillion*, an increase of $70 billion, even with a drop in defense costs and a bad economy. Unlike the real world, government spending is immune to recessions.

This runaway activity is partially due to the system. The basis for the new budget is the old one. The flaws in the previous one are usually not examined or challenged. Typically, the Office of Management and Budget plugs in the old figures and adds the cost of inflation, new programs voted for by Congress, and rises in pensions, benefits, and entitlements, all of which make it *seem* impossible to drastically cut back costs.

From the President's OMB people, the budget goes to the thirteen House Committees for appropriations, then to the Senate Finance Committee. In most cases, the Congressional people, ignorant of the real workings of the flabby, over-budgeted executive agencies, just vote an "okay," adding billions in pork barrel projects for their local constituents as they go.

The budgeteers have even developed a semantic trick to make their growing budgets seem smaller. It is called "Current Services Budget," which means that as entitlements and programs grow at a natural rate, so would the size of the budget. But if they *reduce the growth* somewhat, they claim that the budget has been "cut," even if it is larger than the prior year's.

If one is smart enough to see through that obfuscation (increasingly used by Governors as well), **there is a way to construct a budget that the nation can afford**.

It would require throwing out the old system entirely, then starting all over again. That's the theory of ZBB— Zero-Based Budgeting—a method increasingly called on by hard-pressed private businesses. ZBB doesn't begin with last year's anything. It starts from scratch, as if there were no government, then develops a budget for what is *necessary* to run the operation.

Once that's done, the zero-based budget could be exposed to the public and the media. Simultaneously, the President and the Congress could discuss it, hopefully from the vantage point of the taxpaying citizen. This might be the only way to halt a spend-crazy Congress and a lazy White House, no matter which party is in charge of either.

What would happen if we used ZBB in Washington and examined the *real* needs of each federal agency anew?

Want to hazard a guess? We could probably save $500 billion a year and eliminate the deficit, stop stealing money from the aged (see SOCIAL SECURITY), and reduce taxes to boot.

Anyone for ZBB?

5

BUILDINGS

Like in the Roman Empire?

MAYBE WASHINGTON KNOWS something that has passed most real-estate people by.

While the commercial office building business is in the worst shape in thirty years, the federal government is constructing like mad, expanding its inventory of thousands of buildings. The real-estate section of the Sunday edition of the *New York Times* recently featured a story on the government building boom in Washington and even Philadelphia. Bureaucrats everywhere like to build, but it's an obsession with the U.S. government.

When a developer in the private sector decides to construct an office building, he has to worry about costs, overruns, overtime, depreciation, taxes, then finally the state of the economy and his ability to rent the building.

The General Services Administration, which handles our government buildings, has no such worries. They merely build, often with overruns, then automatically "rent" the space to federal agencies, regardless of any market climate.

The GSA presently holds 15 million square feet of vacant space in thousands of federal buildings. Still, they're on their usual construction spree. This is in addition to the $2 billion the government spent in 1992

21

to lease office space in private buildings all over the nation.

Under the budget heading "New Construction" are more than 50 entries that add up to $5 billion.

The projects include: a new $22 million lab for the U.S. Geological Survey; a $38 million FBI field office; a $50 million Department of Transportation headquarters; a $25 million U.S. Courthouse in Louisiana; a $182 million Federal Building in Boston; a $21 million dollar Courthouse in Prince Georges County in the Washington suburb; a $69 million Federal Building and Courthouse annex in Minneapolis; a $33 million Courthouse annex in Oregon; an $81 million Federal Building in West Virginia; a new Naval Command Center for a quarter *billion* dollars in Virginia; and so on, and so on.

The GSA spent another billion that year for repairs and alterations, including $1.6 million for Building No. 6 at the World Trade Center—a structure the government doesn't even own.

But the real surprises in this expensive package are the generous building gifts from Uncle Sam to scores of private institutions. They range from the Forestry Science Complex at Northern Arizona University ($4.5 million) to a computer center at Iowa State University ($2.2 million) to a Primate Research Institute in Alamogordo, New Mexico ($4 million), in addition to others for a total of almost $100 million.

When queried about GSA support for these private buildings, a high-ranking official of the General Services Administration was nonplussed.

"I know absolutely nothing about them," he said embarrassed. "These appropriations were passed by Congress and all we do here is write the checks."

But on our bank accounts?

Is there a solution to the irresponsible building frenzy by the government? Yes.

(1) Place a five-year freeze on all new construction.

(2) Outlaw building grants to private organizations.

(3) Follow the suggestion of a government auditor: "Why not," he asked, "take the government employees out of the expensive leased space and move them into the dozens of military installations we're closing down? We'll save a fortune in rent."

Now that's an idea.

6

CARS

Washington on Wheels

THEY MAY NOT CHERISH them as much as they do their private planes, but government executives love driving around in taxpayer-paid cars.

The government owns and operates a vast fleet of 340,000 non-tactical, non-postal motor vehicles—about 190,000 in the civilian agencies and 150,000 in the military. Nowhere among bureaucrats, even in the old USSR, is the perk of a car more valued than in the U.S. government. In fact, there is almost one government car for every ten federal civilian employees—at least ten times the ratio of private corporations.

Many higher-echelon employees may even have someone drive them around. The government Office of Personnel Management lists 12,000 people with the classification of "Driver." Some handle trucks, but many others escort bureaucrats around in a style they were never accustomed to. (See CHAUFFEURS.)

Congress is one agency that's loaded with free cars. Every Representative and Senator is entitled to a leased automobile, with upkeep, and a free parking spot in the Capitol garage. Not only elected officials, but the working brass on the Hill get car freebies. That includes the Postmaster, the House Clerk, the Senate Secretary, the Doorkeeper, the Sergeant-at-Arms, and often their assistants. At $7000 per car per year for a lease and upkeep, Congress eats $4 million a year in this extra waste.

The cost of this government obsession is enormous. It costs $3 billion to buy the vehicles, even with large discounts, and half that just for the civilian cars. The yearly depreciation is $1800 per, or another two-thirds billion dollars. The government admits to a car-upkeep cost of $915 million in 1988, a figure that has now long passed the $1 billion mark. Drivers, with salaries, benefits, and overhead, add another $150 million to the tab.

Overall, keeping the federal employee mobile sets the taxpayer back several billion a year.

Why doesn't the public ever see this enormous fleet of civilian federal cars on the road?

Because they're invisible. Government cars no longer carry official decals on their doors. A General Services Administration spokesman claims they were too hard to remove when the cars were sold. Cynics believe the true reason was to keep voters from first observing, then complaining, about these caravans of waste.

The cars are parked in underground parking garages, outdoor lots, and motor pools all over the country, some of which employ full-time mechanics to handle repairs. Other motor pools are placed in high-rent districts. Even the General Accounting Office, a dedicated federal watchdog, has its own pool of 20 cars right in downtown Washington.

What's wrong with taxis and subways in big cities? And what about cars in the countryside? How many are actually needed?

"The government shouldn't be in the car business as they are," says a General Accounting Office spokesman. "First, they don't need as many cars as they have, and there are much cheaper ways of providing transportation when they do need it. The employee could use his own car and be compensated on a mileage basis. Or, the government could rent cars from Hertz or Avis when they need them. It would save a great deal of money."

Amen.

7

CENSUS

"Count Me, Please!"

WHEN THE CONSTITUTION was written in 1789, the Founding Fathers, in Article I, Section II, Clause III, put in this line: "The actual enumeration [of citizens] shall be made within three years after the first meeting of Congress, and every subsequent ten years in a manner as they shall by law direct."

The requirement was, of course, the Decennial Census, designed to help Congress redistrict our Representatives based on the changing population.

Today, the Founding Fathers wouldn't recognize the Census Bureau. It's now ensconced within the Department of Commerce, and instead of an agency dedicated to counting heads as the Constitution ordered, it has become a giant polling operation. And an inefficient, Big Brother one at that.

The Bureau's main job is a simple one, but apparently too much to ask for, even at the agency's inflated costs. The 1990 Census was considered the worst to date. Local officials howled that they were robbed of constituents, with as many as 8 million people, especially minorities, uncounted.

The Census people, like most federal agencies, like to flex their bureaucratic muscles, even when they're not invited. Every ten years, they force a large number of Americans to complete an expensive "long form," which was never mentioned in the Constitution. Not only do the Census probers ask name and address, but sex, race, income, property, household furnishings, and dozens of other irrelevant and impertinent questions. For those who refuse to answer, the Census people—unlike such pollsters as Roper or Gallup—threaten federal prosecution.

Head counting is part of the Constitution, but this invasion of privacy is not.

To keep busy between each Census, the 2700 employees in the Bureau have taken on other jobs, including counting cars and refrigerators, which are not listed in the Constitution either. These statistics are mainly useful to industry, which can afford to do the research themselves, without taxpayer subsidies. After the Gulf War, the Bureau asked an employee to estimate the number of enemy killed. She did so, but when she divulged the figure, she was told she would be fired. When the incident was reported in the press, the Bureau backed off.

All this extra probing wastes billions. The Census Bureau spends $230 million a year—in addition to the $1.4 *billion* at Census time. The next Census, without accounting for inflation, will cost the taxpayers $3.5 billion altogether, a figure never anticipated—even proportionately—by the Founding Fathers.

The Commerce Department houses a sister organization, the Economic and Statistical Analysis group, which employs 563 people and has an annual budget of $46 million. They provide us with the GNP, the Leading Economic Indicators, the Balance of Payments figures, and regional economic activity.

The solution is simple:

(1) Get the Census Bureau back to its Constitutional

mandate. Cancel their other statistical work, switching only a few important studies to the Economic and Statistical Analysis group.

(2) Stop the Bureau's nosy long-form invasion of our privacy at Census time.

(3) Bring their wasteful cadre of 2700 employees down to a permanent group of 300.

(4) Contract out the year 2000's census to private polling groups who will do a more accurate job for a few hundred million dollars.

(5) Use the $3 billion saved to reduce the federal deficit.

The Census Bureau is the perfect model of Washington waste. Give a government agency a simple job—in this case, counting heads every ten years—and they'll make an expensive, convoluted federal case out of it every time.

8

CHAPLAINS

The High Price of Prayer

No, THIS IS not the Chaplain Corps of the armed services, an old American tradition. This has to do with God and the U.S. Congress.

In the 1960s, the Supreme Court—drawing on the concept of separation of church and state—ruled that not even school children could be led in organized prayer at the beginning of the day. But the United States Congress is apparently immune to the verdicts of the Court and too religious to do without divine counsel.

Each session of the House and the Senate is opened with a prayer. Is it led by a pious member of the body, or some volunteer clergyman—Catholic, Protestant, or Jewish—from the community, hopeful the legislators will see the light during their deliberations?

No, that's too simple. Everything Congress does (and the White House, too, as we shall see) has to cost money, and a lot of it. Both Houses of Congress have their own full-time, salaried Chaplains, at a stiff price to the taxpayers.

The House Chaplain gets a salary of—and this is not a typo—$115,300. Not to be outdone, the Senate Chaplain spends much more per member-soul on his small body of 100 legislators. He receives about the same salary as his

House colleague, but he has an overall budget of $300,000, including pay for secretaries and office space to help him shepherd his sometimes wayward flock.

If it worked, it might be worth the price. But thus far there are no signs of divine intervention in the chambers of the U.S. Congress.

9

CHAUFFEURS AND LIMOUSINES

"Home, James!"

THERE'S NOTHING like a limo. Especially when it's free and chauffeured.

That's the theme song of many high-ranking Washington politicians and bureaucrats who feel like *Ubermenschen* when they're riding in the backseat of a government black Cadillac or Lincoln, with a chauffeur handling the bucking of traffic and a small light at the rear of the limo making it possible for them to do work—or read the latest Redskin scores—as they commute.

We used to laugh when we saw the limousines parade through Spassky Gate on their way into the Kremlin. Now we can see the same sight at the White House any day. The President maintains 29 limousines for himself and the use of his most favored assistants, who bear the unofficial title of "Commissioned Officers."

These are not military men, but Assistants to the President, Deputy Assistants, and Special Assistants. All have access to the White House limos and drivers, which means they can get chauffeurs and cars to take them to lunch or dinner parties, with their "man" waiting outside while they pursue their pleasure.

But among the highest perks in perk-mad Washington is what's called "portal-to-portal" chauffeur and limo, which means you have your own government-paid wheels and driver wherever you go. He picks you up at home in the morning, takes you to work, then to lunch and back, and even—on the sly—conveys your wife while she shops. Then home in the evening, or to a dinner party, or whatever.

Who gets this bizarre, ridiculously anti-democratic (small *d*), and very expensive privilege?

In the House and Senate, chauffeured cars are granted to the Speaker and party chiefs. (See CONGRESS, LEADERS.)

In the Executive Branch, besides the President and the Vice President, the list of people eligible for "home-to-work" chauffeured cars, according to law, includes: all Justices of the Supreme Court; all Cabinet officers; Deputy Cabinet officers; Ambassadors, including the Ambassador to the United Nations; the Secretaries of the various armed services; the Chairman, Vice Chairman, and members of the Joint Chiefs of Staff; Commandant of the Coast Guard; heads of the CIA and FBI; Chairman of the Federal Reserve; Postmaster General; and head of the General Accounting Office.

(Within the armed services, some generals don't believe they need Congress's authorization or instruction from U.S. Code 1344. They just get sergeants to drive them around—anywhere.)

The President has the privilege of naming six of his close White House aides as recipients of "portal-to-portal" service—a prime perk for him to dispense. And according to the 1986 "reform" law, the Chief Executive can also choose ten agency employees for this automotive knighthood.

So far, those lists have included the President's Chief of Staff, his Economic Adviser, the National Security

Adviser and his deputy, the Budget Director and his deputy, the Chief of Protocol, and the AID (Agency for International Development) administrator.

How many "pashas of perk" does that make in all? It's hard to tell. At first glance, it looks like about 50, plus Ambassadors abroad. But that doesn't include members of the Washington Establishment who cheat. A 1983 study found that 190 bureaucrats had chauffeured cars providing them with portal-to-portal service for work and/or pleasure.

What about now? A follow-up General Accounting Office report in 1991, after the number of "portal-to-portal" people was limited by law, showed that the cheating had been reduced, but was still there. Of the 61 people the survey found were being picked up at their homes by a government chauffeur, 29 were in violation of the law.

These included four spouses who used the limo and driver to go to "various locations." Several under-bosses also took illegal advantage of the perk, as did some chauffeurs, who took the cars to their own homes after their night's work was over.

Each of these cars, with cost, depreciation, and chauffeur—who go into overtime at evening affairs—eats up well over $100,000 each. There are also those limos and drivers waiting in the White House pool for the next staffer to feel the urge.

The solution?

(1) No one except the President, Vice President, Speaker of the House, President Pro Tem of the Senate, Secretaries of State, Treasury (surprised?), and Defense—the top six people in line of succession for the Presidency—plus the Chairman of the Joint Chiefs should have chauffeured limousines.

(2) The spare limos, including most of those in the White House motor pool, should be sold and none reordered. All other bureaucrats can drive their own cars, and *if* it's for official business, bill the government 28 cents a mile, the same amount allowed citizens by the IRS.

Not only will it save millions in tax money, but it'll bring some of these *Ubermenschen* down to reality—which is one real broke government.

10

CHIEF EXECUTIVE

No One's In Charge

THE IMAGE of the American President, with his near-regal trappings, elegant mansion, Oval Office, and Air Force One, conjures up a sense of power.

But in reality, his title of "Chief Executive" is a highly misleading one—actually a misnomer. Originally, the President was called the "Chief Magistrate," which is much closer to the semantic mark.

Under no circumstances can he be compared to a chief executive officer in American business. In a corporation, when things are tough, the CEO can get tougher—sell off subsidiaries, fire middle management, close plants, reduce overhead drastically.

Right here, the comparison between an American President and the CEO stops. The occupant of the White House is much weaker, especially when trying to run his "corporation," the federal government.

The President is only truly the Chief Executive when it comes to defense, external affairs, and territorial integrity. There he's on firm footing as Commander-in-Chief of the Armed Forces. Congress likes to remind us that they have the Constitutional right to "declare war." True, but history shows that Presidents are the ones who actually "make war," with or without Congress.

Harry Truman asked no one when he went into Korea; Lincoln raised an army, spent millions, even discarded *habeas corpus* for the first time in history before Congress met in 1861; Andrew Jackson took Florida without Congressional approval, as Thomas Jefferson did when he bought Louisiana. George Bush was already up to his GI boots in the Persian Gulf before Congress reluctantly gave him the okay. American Presidents have involved the nation in hostilities more than 100 times, and Congress has approved a declaration of war only five times.

But when it comes to domestic affairs, the President is nobody's Chief Executive. Maybe that's why so many of them turn to the power arena of foreign concerns. In fact, the President can't really fire anyone except his own Cabinet and a few thousand political appointees—whose jobs must then be refilled anyway. The hole in Presidential power is that once a budget has been settled, the President and the nation are locked in.

That's why veterans of the Washington scene correctly believe that no one is in charge of the government. Inexorably handed a budget larger than the previous year's, each federal bureaucracy, no matter how small or insignificant, is off on a spending spree, with no one, not even the President, to account to. Travel, furniture, supplies, outlays, are the agency's own business and no one else's. The bureaucracy knows that next year another budget, still larger, is on its way.

If power corrupts, then Washington agencies are corrupted absolutely by the absence of a Chief Executive with counterbalancing power. It's as if a private corporation was headed toward bankruptcy and no one was allowed to try to turn it around.

Presidents can, of course, use their persuasive power as a national "bully pulpit" by submitting smaller budgets to Congress to begin with, then use their prestige to try to get the anti-waste measure through. But that has not happened in modern times. Whether a Democrat or Republican is in the Oval Office, Presidential budgets are larger year in and year out.

Yet, in fits of economy, some Presidents have tried to save money and cut waste by *impounding* or *sequestering* funds—that is, not spending what Congress has already appropriated. In this way, they hoped to resemble a true Chief Executive.

But it was not to be.

The last President to lock horns with Congress by impounding money he didn't think necessary was Richard Nixon. That prompted Congressional action to defang the President even further in domestic affairs. In 1974, Congress passed the Budget and Impoundment Control Act, which set up a system to stop any Chief Executive in an economy mood.

Today, a President who wants to "rescind" money already appropriated, has to go to Congress, certifying that the funds are not necessary to fulfill the purpose of the original bill. Congress has 45 days to consider it. If they do nothing, the money has to be spent. If they agree with the President's cuts, or parts of them, they must pass a "recession package" allowing the impoundment.

Senator John McCain of Arizona has been fighting to turn the situation around, to put the onus on Congress to act. Over the last few years, he has offered two amendments that would allow the President to impound any appropriation *unless* Congress passed a resolution stopping him. The first was badly defeated, but in 1992, the vote on the McCain amendment was much closer on the Senate floor, giving heart to those who want to strengthen the Oval Office in domestic matters.

Stymied at impounding funds, the hapless President may have only one other option. He can contemplate vetoing part of the appropriation without having to reject the whole bill. This last-ditch effort is called the "Line Item Veto" (see that listing), but it has never been used in American history. If it is ever operational, it will be the President's final chance to become what he's already glibly, if falsely, called: the nation's Chief Executive.

Meanwhile, rest assured that no one, but no one, is in charge in the nation's capital.

11

CONGRESS, LEADERS

Life at the Top

IMAGINE A DINING ROOM that holds twenty, with privileged guests seated around a long graceful table set with fine china and silver. At the head of the table is an elected official of the United States government. A chef, on the government payroll, has cooked a splendid French meal. And, naturally, the taxpayers are picking up the tab.

The White House?

Not really. This dining room on the first floor of the House side of the Capitol building flanks the prosaic chamber where ordinary Congressmen eat. It belongs to the Speaker of the House, and he entertains whomever he wants for lunch or dinner. His chef also works for the members' restaurant, but that salary appears nowhere in the printed House budget.

In the perk scandal that rocked the House, not only was the gustatory tidbit of the Speaker's Dining Room overlooked, but so was the entire size and upkeep of what is loosely called "The Congressional Leadership."

In the House, the leadership begins with the Speaker, but includes the Majority Leader, the Majority Whip, and the Chief Deputy Majority Whip. On the other side of the aisle there are three more—the Minority Leader, the Minority Whip, and the Chief Deputy Minority Whip.

Except for the Speaker's, are the jobs just extra burdens they have to carry? Hardly. All seven "officials," six of whom are named by their party peers, receive extra compensation from the government, separate offices in addition to their regular Congressional suites, and staffs so large that they defy explanation.

The Speaker has a spacious suite of offices on the second floor of the Capitol, which includes the Rayburn Room, an enormous, beautifully furnished chamber that resembles a ballroom and is used for official receptions. The Speaker's staff includes twenty-one employees, in addition to the twenty he has in his regular Congressional office in the Longworth House Office Building.

However, the Speaker is outclassed by the Majority Leader of the House, whose entourage takes on almost Presidential proportions. He has twenty-seven employees, including two press people and three full-time foreign-policy advisers. As part of his annual million-dollar expenditure, some $30,000 is spent on refreshments for meetings alone. In his regular Congressional Office, there are another nineteen employees.

The third man in the hierarchy, the Majority Whip, has fifteen employees, and spends closer to $40,000 a year entertaining his colleagues with sandwiches, yogurt, croissants, et cetera. One extraordinary expense by the Whip is a "speechwriter." (So he can make speeches to whom?)

Going down the line, the Chief Deputy Majority Whip has six employees and an official suite.

The Minority Leaders in the House duplicate that excess, but being out of power, their ranks are smaller. The Minority Leader has twenty-three employees, including two press people; the Minority Whip has thirteen; and the Chief Deputy Minority Whip only two.

The top people in the hierarchy not only have free cars, as do all Congressmen, but they are provided with chauffeurs as well. (News flash! The Minority Whip has embarrassedly given up his driver.) A search of the House Clerk's report turns up, in the "Miscellaneous" section, the listing of leases for these official vehicles. But the drivers are mentioned nowhere.

"Who drives the Speaker?" I asked a spokesman in his office.

"Oh, that's a Capitol police sergeant," he responded. From the Clerk's office I learned that the same is true of the other leaders, each of whom has a Capitol cop serving as his chauffeur. That conveniently permits the cost to be buried, away from prying eyes.

The practice of a separate office for the Speaker is surely legal, for he is a government official elected by the entire House. In fact, he comes directly after the Vice President in line of succession for the Presidency.

But the other leaders, while traditional, are all partisan people elected only by their own party. Not only do the Democratic and Republican leaders have large staffs of their own, as we've seen, but party workers in the House Democratic Steering Committee, the House Democratic Caucus, and the Republican Conference are all on the government payroll, which sounds mightily like a violation of the Constitution.

Millions of Americans are not registered as either Democrats or Republicans, and the one-person-one-vote concept may well be violated by the federal subsidy of specific "party jobs" in the House and Senate. In the House alone, the party groups—in addition to the "majority" and "minority" staffs—have fifty employees on the payroll. With expenses, that costs us $2.5 million a year.

The House leadership is virtually duplicated in the Senate. Together, they represent extravagant operations that call for streamlining, in personnel, overhead, and perks.

What's the solution?

(1) First, we can surely do without the Speaker's Dining Room.

(2) Capitol cops should not be hidden drivers. If the leaders can stand the scrutiny of hiring chauffeurs, let them be listed in the budget.

(3) The staffs of the leadership are outrageously bloated—162 in all—and should be cut in half or more.

(4) And last, but not least, someone ought to look into the practice of taxpayers picking up the tab for political party workers on the federal payroll. Congress, after all, is supposed to be the legislature of *all* the people.

True reform of that not-so-august-body, if it is ever to come, can only begin from the top down.

12

CONGRESSIONAL COMMITTEES

Washington's Growth Industry

OVER THE PAST THREE DECADES, the fastest growing business on Capitol Hill has been the House and Senate committees and their staffs.

Up through the early 1960s, Capitol Hill was a reasonably well-functioning community with powerful committee chairmen and a small group of staffers who kept the legislative machine well oiled. But there was a problem.

Critics complained that the committees were in the grip of tough old-timers, who used their seniority to keep a lid on young members chafing for power. The Young Turks finally got their way in the 1970s when the "Watergate Babies" were elected in the aftermath of that debacle. The result was the quashing of the oligarchy.

In its place, we now have anarchy.

Today, there are approximately 300 committees in the House and Senate, including standing, select, and joint committees, and their proliferating subcommittees, each with its own chairman, staff, office, and perks. The promise of "Every man a King" has not been accomplished in society, but it is true in the marble halls of Congress.

Since there are only 535 members, more than half of them are "in power." Local wags say: "If you recognize a Congressman but don't know his name, just call him 'Mr.

Chairman.' The chances are that you'll be right, and you'll have pleased him right off the bat."

The cost of all this is phenomenal, especially in the growing numbers of well-paid committee staffers, who earn up to $112,000 a year, according to the House Finance Committee.

In 1950, the entire House Committee staff numbered 180. By the time of John Kennedy's administration in the early 1960s, there were still only 700 staff members in the House and Senate combined. That number is now 3700, a fivefold increase in 30 years—a period when the population of the country grew only 37%. Congress has been twelve times swifter than the people.

Little wonder that in 1992, without adding a single new Representative, the House budget went up 20%, pushing overall Congressional expenditures past $3 billion.

(If Presidential advocates are chortling, please see WHITE HOUSE STAFF, which has the same unenviable record.)

The solution is simple.

Cut out half the committees, chairmen, and staffs. It will save the taxpayers at least $250 million and Congress's work will be streamlined—if that's possible.

No, we don't have to return to the seniority system, but a few steps backward into sanity wouldn't hurt.

13

CONGRESSMEN, PERSONAL STAFF

An Army of Their Own

WHILE OUR ATTENTION was hypnotically focused on bounced checks and House perks, the big-money waste in Congress was going unnoticed.

The U.S. Congress—both the House and the Senate—has a payroll of more than 20,000 employees for only 535 members, a ridiculously disproportionate and expensive ratio. As we've seen, 3700 of them are committee staffers, but the bulk of the others make up the personal staffs of the Congressmen.

We're talking about a small army: 7800 people in the House and 4000 in the Senate, a total of almost 12,000 federal employees. They're quite well paid: an AA (Administrative Assistant) for a Congressman earns as much as $102,000. The cost to taxpayers, with salaries, benefits, office space, overhead, et cetera, runs to about a *billion and a half* dollars a year.

It wasn't always that way. Back in FDR's time, when legislation was spewing out of Congressmen's offices at a record pace (FDR vetoed 635 bills), each Representative had only two aides. By Truman's time it had grown to a still-reasonable five. And today? Each Representative is allowed eighteen full-time and four part-time aides, an excessive, near-royal entourage.

And how about the Senate? That's much worse. Each Senator has 40 aides, not counting those on his committees.

Don't these large staffs help the Representatives and Senators do a better job? At face value, it would seem so, but some observers, including this one, believe they're actually an obstacle to smoothly functioning democracy. Instead of a shirtsleeve legislator, the Congressman or Congresswoman is set up as an over-busy, over-revered figurehead more involved in meetings, speeches, and reports than in the nitty-gritty of direct representation. As his personal army grows, so does his distance from his constituents.

The growth of staff—personal and committee—has also pushed Congress into looking for still more space, which costs money. In addition to the three House Office Buildings (Cannon, Rayburn, and Longworth) and three Senate Buildings (Hart, Dirksen, and Russell), Congress has taken over two more buildings near the Capitol and renamed them after recent leaders: the O'Neill House Office Building (in honor of former Speaker Thomas P. "Tip" O'Neill II), and the Ford House Office Building (in honor of former President Gerald Ford, who came up through the House Republican leadership).

Besides the Washington office, each Congressman also has up to three offices in the home district. Counting rent, telephone, and staff, these 1000-plus local offices all over the nation cost an estimated $30 million a year.

What's the answer to this crush of bureaucrats around our Congressmen? Simple.

It requires no argument or sophistry. One district office is enough for any Congressman. The others should be closed. The personal staffs, like the committee staffs, should be cut in half, for several reasons:

(1) It will halt the continuous real-estate expansion on Capitol Hill.

(2) It will bring the Congressman's focus down to size so that he can better identify with the people instead of acting like the manager of a large government enterprise.

(3) Most important, it will save at least a half billion dollars a year.

14

CONSULTANTS

The Shadow Empire

"THERE'S A SHADOW FEDERAL GOVERNMENT —one nobody ever sees. It's a secret empire that's costing the taxpayers a fortune, somewhere between $4.5 and $20 billion a year. And no one's trying to bring it under control."

That statement from a staff member of the Senate Governmental Affairs Committee is an eye-opener, even for experienced Washington watchers.

"I'm talking about the outside consulting industry which feeds off the bureaucracy," he continues. "It's a fiction that the government is limited to government employees. There are thousands of people in the Beltway who are making a lot of money by being contract consultants to the federal agencies. Some consultants—like lawyers—are getting $1000 a day, and the taxpayers are footing the bill."

The use of outside consultants, from scientists to accountants, fits the Beltway appetite for high life-style and less work for government employees. And it's only now beginning to be uncovered.

"We got a request from the Senate Governmental Affairs Committee, Federal Services Subcommittee, to check into this consulting business," says an evaluator of the General Accounting Office. "They suspected too much money was being spent on outside consulting and wanted us to check into it. First, we found out that there were about 3500 people with regular consulting appointments who were getting $35 million a year. But that was small stuff. Then we turned to the outside consulting *contracts*. There we learned that an unreported fortune was being spent."

How did the auditors find out that billions were slipping through the government's fingers?

"Well, it turned out that the government agencies were simply lying," says the GAO auditor. "They have to check a box which asks if the order is for a consultant. They were saying 'No' even if the real answer was 'Yes.' They admitted to a few hundred million dollars of consultant use, but we learned the truth by checking the object class analysis number on each account. When the tally came in, we found that in one recent fiscal year, they had spent $4.9 *billion* on outside consultants of every kind. In fact, I'll fax you the report."

The list is overwhelming. Defense was the biggest spender, but not the only one by far: $40 million in consultants were contracted for by HUD (Housing and Urban Development); $308 million by the Agency for International Development; $47 million by Interior; $43 million by Treasury; $44 million by Commerce; $56 million by the Federal Emergency Management Agency (some management!); $20 million by Labor; $12 million by the TVA (Tennessee Valley Authority); $99 million by Energy; and even $60 million by Education, consulting advice that has obviously gone to waste.

"This scandal—without the details we now have—came to Jimmy Carter's attention back in the 1970s," says the Senate committee spokesman. "He got riled up, but after a while, Carter got nowhere and gave up the fight. When Reagan came into the White House, he also got angry about the outside consultants, but he gave up too. Both Presidents were defeated by the entrenched bureaucracy. There's a feeling in the agencies that what they do is nobody's business. They laugh at the idea of oversight, and just do what they please—including hiring consultants for virtually everything. And the situation is getting worse. We came up with a $4.9 billion figure, but I think that's understated. It could be as much as $20 billion."

As an example of the widespread abuse, he explained that the government has a legion of lawyers on its regular payroll—14,492 to be exact—but the agencies still use an enormous amount of $150-an-hour legal help from outside law firms. "From what I can see, the government attorneys mainly manage the work of the outside law firms the government hires as consultants."

What can be done to stop this wasteful abuse?

"It's really simple," says the committee spokesman. "Instead of getting angry, all Jimmy Carter or Reagan had to do was sign an Executive Order outlawing all consulting contracts. It would be finished instantly. Any agency person who broke the order would be violating the 'Anti-Deficiency Act,' which states that a federal employee cannot illegally obligate the government. All this President, or any other one, has to do to save billions is to make that stroke of his pen."

We're still waiting.

15

DECORATING AND FURNITURE

Herman Miller, Anyone?

How much could the federal government possibly spend on decorating?

Much more than you, or I, or any reasonable person, could imagine.

When we think of government furniture, we conjure up images of chipped metal desks and 1950s vinyl-covered chairs in Post Offices or Social Security bureaus.

Think again. That's a smoke screen so we won't think about the expensively decorated federal offices—complete with Herman Miller desks, rugs, and the latest built-in wall systems—that have been refurbished at some bureaucrat's whim. That's closer to the truth.

A few years ago, an intrepid reporter for the *Washington Post* broke a scandal. The government was spending $250 million a year on furniture, he learned, while a government warehouse in Franconia, Virginia, held a giant cache of perfectly good furniture.

Have things gotten any better? Hardly. In fact, they're much worse. The U.S. government is spending considerably more than $250 million a year on office furniture, and even more than anyone in the government knows about. It is a scandal waiting to be born.

Are there any controls on such spending? The answer

is simply "No." Then who's to stop a ranking bureaucrat from spending $100,000 redoing his already resplendent office? No one. The decision to buy furniture is made by individual agencies, not any central group. They can refurnish all or part of their offices—whether they're moving or staying put—without a decision from the White House or even the General Services Administration, which some government people mistakenly believe is in charge.

Actually, no one is in charge. As we have seen in the section BUDGET, the previous year's appropriation goes up inexorably. This applies to furniture and supplies, and nothing is reduced just because a large amount of money may have already been spent on refurnishing the year before. There's always a small fortune available for government agencies to buy whatever they want, and there's no one to ask or check with.

All the General Services Administration does is set up advance price contracts with hundreds of suppliers for everything from wooden desks to pictures. But the bureaucrats do the deciding and the buying on their own— the old system of foxes guarding the hen house. In fact, if they want, they can entirely bypass the GSA and buy through other suppliers. It's that system that allowed one Congressional leader to pay over $3000 for a single desk.

How much does the government actually spend on furniture and decorating each year?

"No one in the government really knows," says a top GSA spokesman. "We know how much the agencies spend when they use our contract system. But that doesn't include the Department of Defense, who mainly do their own buying, and even agencies who don't like what's available from our suppliers. All I can find out for you is how much money went through our contract system."

I asked him to find out his end, and after a computer run, he did. The figure turned out to be *$676 million* just in fiscal 1991! He agreed that estimating that to be half the true total would be conservative. More liberally, it would be three times as much.

$1.35 to $2 billion a year on new furniture and decorating?

That's right, and there's no cutback or stopping point in sight. Where does that show in the federal budget? Nowhere. There's no such listing as "Furniture" or "Decorating" in the hefty document. As we shall see in OVERHEAD, budget items are not clearly stated, on purpose. The government plays cat and mouse with the taxpayer whenever it can.

What happens to all the old furniture that's replaced? Does it go to the warehouse?

Not usually. Now, it's mainly given away. Another GSA spokesman tried to explain that system.

"When an agency wants to get rid of furniture, we offer it for 30 days to other federal agencies, who can get it free of charge if they pay for transportation. Then we offer it to state and municipal agencies. After that, we donate it to charity."

What about the furniture that's in the warehouse? Do government people first have to check it out before they buy new stuff?

"No, they don't," this spokesman explained. "But now we're trying to refinish the wood stuff and reupholster the chairs and couches so that more government agencies will want them. But no federal agency has to take the furniture if they don't want to."

Want to?

That phrase perfectly expresses the wasteful privilege Washington bureaucrats have to spend billions of our tax money on decorating and new furniture that *nobody* will ever know if they actually need.

Did they say almost $2 billion for furnishings in one year? That's more than the entire budget of the state of North Dakota.

16

ELECTRICITY, FEDERAL

We're Lighting Up Las Vegas

IN NEW YORK, Connecticut, and New Jersey, customers pay heavily for their power, as high as 12 cents a kilowatt hour.

But if we go out West, where the government-owned Hoover Dam sits astride the Colorado River, we find that a kilowatt of federal power is sold to local organizations for only a penny. The lucky beneficiaries can leave the lights on all night without worrying. Uncle Sam is paying.

The government hydroelectric program, whose power comes from hundreds of dams built with public money, is a perfect example of the irrationality of much of our federal government. We all pay, but only selected people benefit.

The multi-billion-dollar bill for the dams goes to every taxpayer, but only 6% of the nation receives cheap federal electricity in return.

The Western Area Power Administration, which distributes the electricity in that part of the country, gets it mainly from the dams along the Colorado River—the Hoover, the Parker, the Glen Canyon, and others—then "wholesales" it to customers in their area. In Nevada, the town of Boulder City, about twenty miles from Vegas, is one beneficiary of this federal bounty. It pays only 1.2 cents a kilowatt and resells it to citizens for 3.6 cents, about a third of what Northeastern and Midwestern voters have to pay for their electricity.

Surprisingly, this taxpayer subsidy goes not only to co-ops and municipalities, but to profit-making utilities as well, all at the same cheap price.

In the early 1980s, Congresswoman Barbara Boxer of California started what is known in hydroelectric circles as the "Boxer Rebellion." She suggested that the government auction off the power of the Hoover Dam at market rates. Others suggested that the dams be sold to utilities, but all were shouted down. Right now, the five federal "power administrations" still owe the Treasury over $10 billion, which they are paying back at a subsidized 3.25% interest rate, while the government borrows at 8%—a giant yearly loss for taxpayers.

One result is a strange situation in which private companies pay a pittance for federal electricity, generally a third of what it costs to make it themselves.

"We get about 13% of all our electricity from Hoover Dam and from the Western Area Power Administration," says a spokesman for the Nevada Power Company, which supplies southern Nevada, including Las Vegas, the largest city in the state. "We pay about a penny per kilowatt, which cuts our costs down a lot. Our own power costs us about 3 cents to produce. So our rate of 5.6 cents a kilowatt to customers is a lot lower than the rest of the country."

Nevada Power, like several utilities in the nation, is getting a taxpayer subsidy in the form of cheap federal electricity. It keeps some and passes on the rest to local customers—including hundreds of well-lit Las Vegas gambling casinos—all courtesy of Uncle Sam.

So the next time you go to Vegas and stroll leisurely down the gaily lit Strip, remember that you're about to lose twice. Once at the slots, and the second time when you realize that it's *your* electricity that's lighting up the night.

17

"ESSENTIAL AIR"

Flying Out of Control

SAY YOU WANT to go skiing in Vermont—Killington or Pico, to be specific.

Before January 1992, you'd have to fly from Newark Airport or Boston to nearby Lebanon, New Hampshire. The cost? On Precision Air, which is part of Northwest Airlines, a regular round tripper from Newark would cost you $253 with seven days' notice. Then once you got there, you'd drive 45 miles to your ski resort.

Well, that's all changed now. Life has been made easy for the weary skier. All you have to do is get on Skymaster, a small airline, at Newark, pay only $99 round trip (or a super-bargain $78 from Boston), and fly to Rutland, Vermont. That's within an easy twenty-minute drive of the Killington and Pico slopes.

How come the cheap rates and short drive?

Well, simply put, Uncle Sam is so worried about you that he's picking up the tab for your skiing trip. As part of the Department of Transportation's "Essential Air Service," the government subsidizes small airlines to fly into towns that are considered off the beaten path, which is defined as 45 miles from a scheduled airline.

What does it cost the taxpayer to help affluent skiers with cheap flights to "out-of-the-way" Killington?

Skymaster had a total of 370 passengers in March 1992 on its subsidized flights to Rutland, Vermont, and Keene and Laconia, New Hampshire, from Newark and Boston. For that, they received $108,000, or $290 a passenger from the government, or a total of $1,295,762 a year. That means that the skier from the metro areas paid only 25% of his ticket's real cost and Uncle Sam picked up the rest. Meanwhile, of course, Northwest—which is unsubsidized—lost a lot of business.

The Essential Air Service program, which sets back the taxpayers $38 million a year, was put into force by Congress in 1978 when the airlines were deregulated. Representatives feared that if towns were too small and distant from scheduled airline hubs, no one would fly there unless Washington paid the bill.

In some cases, as in the wide open spaces of Montana or Alaska, it might make some sense, but in most cases it is simply a flagrant boondoggle.

One "essential" flight is from Washington, D.C., to the luxurious Homestead resort in Hot Springs, Virginia. The hotel, which charges $335 a day, has one of the richest clientele in the world, including businessmen, conventioneers, Washington politicians, lawyers, and lobbyists.

Before Uncle Sam spent $532,327 to entice National Capital Airways to supply this service, vacationers had to drive 45 miles from Lewisburg, West Virginia. "We couldn't afford to fly them to Hot Springs if not for the government money," says a spokesman for the airline. "There just aren't enough passengers."

Each subsidized trip depletes the Treasury by a different amount. For example, it costs Uncle Sam $205 a passenger so that people from Jackson, Michigan, don't have to drive to the Lansing airport 42 miles away. But that pales beside the $330 per passenger the government pays to put Lewiston, Maine, people in the air. Otherwise they face the great auto trek to Portland, 39 miles away.

The real record in this asinine practice of the Department of Transportation goes to Hutchinson and Parsons, Kansas, where the government kicks in $450 and $585 respectively to spare each passenger the drive to Wichita or Joplin, a distance of 50 or 60 miles.

What's the overall record for this peculiar form of federal welfare?

Perhaps Beloit, Wisconsin, where federal taxpayers shell out $633 for each passenger to subsidize an airline that will save them the travail of driving 47 miles to the Madison airport, the very same distance the unsubsidized residents of Westport, Connecticut, drive to reach JFK airport in New York.

What should be done with EAS?

(1) The first step, of course, is to eliminate the obvious vacation dodges like resorts, ski areas, beaches— subsidizing airlines to fly people to Hot Springs, Virginia; Cape May, New Jersey; Bar Harbor, Maine; and Hyannis, Massachusetts, as we now do.

(2) Close down the whole program. Failing that, to change the distance requirement to 125 miles. That would eliminate most of the EAS service, yet still keep truly isolated Americans from having to drive too far to catch a scheduled plane.

Heaven forbid.

18

EXECUTIVES, FEDERAL

So Many Chiefs

WASHINGTON IS executive green pastures.

While middle management in private industry suffered enormous pain as their ranks were cut back during the recession, things have never been better for the managers of the free-spending federal government.

Even states and municipalities, still a little responsive to the voter, retrenched, especially at their management levels.

But there was no recession in Washington, where the Beltway might as well be as distant from the American people as Tibet. Since there's no "bottom line" in government, there were no cutbacks and no awareness that the nation could no longer afford the bloated legions of federal executives. In fact, the ranks of government managers—237,000 strong, according to the Office of Personnel Management—held steady, perhaps even rose a touch, during the difficult 1990–92 period.

Washington bureaucracy is plainly top heavy. The government doesn't pay the million-dollar salaries of private industry, but they make up for it in the number of executives, assistants, and secretarial backup.

Nominally, there is one executive for every eight employees, a ratio that would bankrupt many private industries. But that number is still understated. In addition to the "manager" category, there are many upper-level "specialists," who, while they may not formally manage, are as well paid and carry as much overhead baggage.

Almost all of them—116,000 to be exact—are professional attorneys, scientists, mathematicians, engineers, accountants, and others who would be considered executives in private industry.

These specialists are in the "GS" white-collar system, which goes from GS-1 (clerks) to GS-3 (beginning secretaries), through GS-13 to GS-15—high-level people who make up to $84,000 a year, plus the government's extraordinary benefits. (See FEDERAL EMPLOYEES, BENEFITS and PENSIONS, FEDERAL EMPLOYEES.)

After the GS ranks, we move to the government's Senior Executive Service, where the pay scale is even higher: $90,000 up to $112,000 for grades ES-1 to ES-6. The highest level government people, on its "Executive Schedule," are paid $104,800 to $143,800.

How can Washington save money here?

Simply by doing what many corporations have done in order to safeguard their profits: eliminate at least 20% of middle managers on the federal payroll.

The saving, with salaries, pension liabilities, overhead, and assistants, would run *$10 billion* a year, a nice beginning toward a more balanced federal budget.

And, sad to state, the citizens would never miss them, or even know they had left.

19

FARMERS, LOANS

You're Paying Heavily for Nostalgia

WHAT IF you had a $300,000 loan with your $400,000 house as collateral and you couldn't make the payments?

Well, that answer is pretty easy. The bank would foreclose and sell the house, probably for $300,000, and you'd end up with nothing.

But, if you were a farmer in the Great Plains, your life story would be quite different.

The Farmers Home Administration, which has loaned billions out to farmers who used their homes, farms, and livestock as collateral, received unusual instructions from Congress as part of the Agricultural Credit Act of 1987. They were to call farmers in and discuss their finances. If they thought a farmer *really* couldn't pay the loan, they would simply forgive part, or even all of it. Not just put a moratorium on payments, but write it down, or write it off as a bad loan.

The house and farm? Of course, he would lose that. Right?

No, he'd keep it all, courtesy of the American taxpayer, especially the suckers in the suburbs and cities who've been unwittingly supporting this fiscal nonsense, to the tune of scores of billions of dollars.

"The farmers who paid their loans off on a regular basis

to the Farmers Home Administration were screwed—
they have to just keep on paying," says a General Accounting Office official who specializes in the farm area.
"But those who were delinquent had their loans written
down quite a bit, or even excused completely. It didn't
pay to keep up the payments."

Did that mean that the farmers' credit was ruined and
they couldn't borrow money again from Uncle Sam?

"Oh, no, they just started all over again and were given
new loans," says the somewhat disgusted auditor.

The extent of the write-downs and write-offs is a national disgrace that has been heavily under-reported by
the press. The billions lost by the taxpayer are testimony
to the power of the farm lobby, whose strength is exaggerated in Congress because under-populated farm states
have the same number (two) of Senators as densely popu-
lated industrial states—the compromise that permitted
the Constitution to be ratified 200 years ago.

In the battle with their urban and suburban cousins the
farmers win out every time. The cost of subsidized loans
to farmers, much of which can never be collected, is
enormous. The Inspector General of the Department of
Agriculture, in his late-1991 report to Congress, details
some of the startling, and dismaying, case histories.

This is not penny-ante activity, but a massive loss to the
taxpayer. The IG correctly calls the Farmers Home Administration "the largest direct lending institution in the
Federal Government." It has a loan portfolio of some *$56
billion*, which has more than doubled in the past five
years, and maintains 2200 offices to service its grateful
clients.

The IG examined 45 farmer-borrowers who had trou-
ble paying their loans and found that they owed Uncle
Sam $79 million, or $1.8 million each. What happened

when they couldn't pay? The loans were permanently reduced $64 million—*an outright gift of $1.4 million to each farmer!*

These figures show the extent to which waste and foolishness are woven into the government farm system. Estimates of the write-offs by the FmHA are about $10 billion.

"The entire program of federal aid to the farmer is not a food-production project," says a GAO official. "It's a social program to keep the 'family farmer' on the farm. And today, courtesy of Uncle Sam, he's often a pretty rich one. Just the tractors of some of these people can cost up to a half million dollars."

The Farmers Home Administration not only underwrites loans for farmers, but for rural homeowners as well. Some mortgages are so heavily subsidized that homeowners pay as low as 1% interest, which means the carrying charges on an $80,000 mortgage are $65 a month!

This contrasts sharply with the behavior of the FHA, which guarantees homeowner mortgages in the suburbs and cities. The FHA home buyer pays approximately market rates for his mortgage, gets no subsidy, and is quickly removed from his home when payments stop.

What can the nation do to rid itself of this yoke called the Farmers Home Administration?

(1) Simply explain to Congress that we have *no nostalgia* for the "family farmer," especially when he's rich enough to owe Uncle Sam almost $2 million and get most of it forgiven.

(2) No new loans should be issued by the FmHA. Farm loans should be obtained the same way someone gets a loan on a business or a regular mortgage on a home.

(3) The entire loan operation should be phased out and the "paper" sold to commercial financial institutions.

(4) The interest-rate subsidies offered to farmers and rural homeowners should be, on a population basis, no more than those offered to city and suburban people.

(5) Congressmen from the non-farm states should organize in bipartisan "city and suburb caucuses" to defeat the farm lobby and their waste of our hard-earned billions. So far, no one has come up with a Suburban Mortgage Relief Act to excuse or write-down those loans.

Isn't it time to save the hundreds of billions in welfare we've been giving away to a million farm families at the expense of the other 120 million?

Nostalgia is a nice emotion, and picture postcards of the family farm with the picket fence framing a field of waving corn are pleasant to look at.

But we may not enjoy the bucolic scene when we learn how much we're paying to have it painted.

20

FARMERS, SUBSIDIES

Welfare on the Great Plains

IN 1980, in response to criticism that the rich among the farmers were getting richer courtesy of Uncle Sam, Congress passed a law limiting subsidy payments to $50,000 per individual.

Now, twelve years later, how has the law been working?

"Some producers continue to reorganize their farms to circumvent the $50,000 payment limit," says the Inspector General of the Department of Agriculture. "Although Congress tried to close payment-limit loopholes by setting new rules in 1987, those new rules appear to have created their own loopholes."

The result is that the largest and wealthiest of farmers continue to receive the major harvest of taxpayer money. One farm consisting of 18 partners received *$600,000* in subsidy payments, regretfully points out the IG.

These subsidies are called "deficiency payments," a government euphemism for checks. The amount is arrived at by subtracting the mythical "target price" for, say, a bushel of wheat, from the actual "market price," which the farmer would get if he were to sell it. The farmer can get the difference in cash, or sell his whole crop at the "target price" to the government, who then pays to store it before giving it away.

The flood of money racing from the cities to the few remaining American farms has not been dammed. It continues through a variety of programs designed to keep the 2.2 million farmers, only half of whom are full-time and less than 500,000 of whom run ongoing commercial farms, happy.

How much have the various farm programs, at least a half dozen in all, cost the American taxpayer and consumer?

In 1986, the cost of the subsidy program alone reached $26 billion. The sum is less today, about $8 billion, but that's only part of the farm-welfare equation. And that amount could skyrocket back any day based on world commodity prices. One estimate is that federal aid to farmers since 1980 has cost the taxpayer $190 billion in direct money.

The indirect cost has been in higher food prices, a punch in the consumer's stomach. The Department of Agriculture estimated in 1989 that food prices were 12% more than they would be if Washington were not meddling in the food market.

One of the most abrasive programs in the farm-welfare armamentium is the "0–92" scheme, a true farmer dole. It is a bizarre federal idea that allows a farmer not to work, not to plant *at all*, and live as well as he ever did. Naturally, courtesy of the taxpayer.

The Congressional Budget Office explains this affront to the middle-class person's struggle for survival. "Current law allows participants in U.S. Department of Agriculture price- and income-support programs to receive 92 percent of their deficiency [subsidy] payments even though . . . they do not plant any of the program crop (the 0–92 program available for wheat and feed grain producers)."

This money-for-no-crop-or-work concept is part of the conservation program to keep some lands idle, a plan that has put 61 million acres—the size of Indiana and Ohio combined—to "sleep" under federal cash protection. Meanwhile, foreign food exporting nations have *increased* their acreage more than that. (The wily French, who are taking foreign markets away from Americans, pay their farmers a subsidy for *extra* production.)

Another penalty for this Washington intervention is unintended. Says Congressman Dick Armey of Texas: "Programs that pay farmers not to farm often devastate rural areas. The reductions hurt everyone from fertilizer companies to tractor salesmen. According to the Department of Agriculture, policies to reduce acreage cost the rural economy 300,000 jobs, and cost the 'farm input' industry $4 billion in lost sales in 1987 alone."

What's behind all this? The federal official involved in auditing the farm program who postulated that the federal scheme was really a "social" one, adds that much of it is also "political."

"The politicians in the farm areas are desperately trying to keep their constituents in business and happy, and they seem to be successful at it," he states candidly.

The reality is that American farmers (a) keep leaving the farm, (b) are consolidating into larger, more economic units, and (c) need disaster relief when crops go bad.

Considering this, what should be done to save billions and still keep the best farmers in business?

(1) The federal government should phase out *all* farm subsidies. (See HONEY; MILK; and WOOL.) The process should take five years to help them adjust to separation from Mother Washington.

(2) The 0–92 program, as the Congressional Budget Office suggests, should be eliminated—immediately.

(3) Close the loopholes of the loopholes in the $50,000 subsidy limit and get the rich planters out of our pocket. One loophole still permits "individuals" to get a second $50,000 if they have "stock" interest in two other farms.

(4) Keep federal crop insurance to protect farmers in case of such natural disasters as floods and drought. Presently the farmer pays 75% and the government 25% of the premium. Reverse that ratio, except for big farmers. It's a small enough price to pay for the end of the fiscal farm disaster.

(5) Furlough off, as gently as possible, the army of farm watchers in the Department of Agriculture, who will no longer be needed.

The overall savings? At least $30 billion a year, plus lower food prices.

And to coin a phrase, that ain't hay.

21

FEDERAL COMMUNICATIONS COMMISSION

How to "Beam Out" Billions

"THE WAY we did it made no sense. It lost billions for the government."

An official of the Federal Communications Commission was talking about one of the largest giveaways in the history of the Republic.

The people own all the airwaves, technically referred to as "the radio spectrum," which means all forms of communications—from radio to television to cellular telephones to satellite transmissions. The range runs from 550 kilohertz (or cycles per second) all the way up to 20 billion cycles, or 20 gigahertz.

"The cellular telephones are in the 800 megahertz [800 million] range," says the spokesman, "and over the last number of years, we have been awarding licenses for their use."

The top 20 major markets were awarded after so-called "comparative hearings." Those who gained a cellular license paid no substantial fee or any royalty to the government. But there were a total of 1460 cellular telephone licenses to award, in 730 metro and rural areas.

How did the government decide to dispense them?

Through a *lottery* among anyone who applied and paid the $200 fee.

The lottery has been held, and many people who won have already sold their federal franchises for fortunes to cellular companies in the field.

Did Uncle Sam get any part of the profit? Naturally not.

But the most traumatic part of the senseless giveaway is that the franchises could just as easily have been auctioned off, as we do with oil drilling rights, which bring in billions.

How much was the giveaway worth?

"We figure that the rural licenses are worth $100 for every person in the area, and $150 per person in the metro ones," explained the FCC spokesman.

What does that come to? A little arithmetic goes a long way when dealing with Uncle Sam. By using a $125 average figure, and with a population of 255 million Americans, we come up with the amount of money the FCC, and its Congressional and White House masters, voluntarily—even enthusiastically—gave away.

How much is it? *$32 billion!*

But that's only the beginning. The FCC is already contemplating its next giveaway. It is called "PCS," or Personal Communication Systems, which occupies the radio spectrum above the cellular telephones, at about the 2 gigahertz level. Within that range there will be space for the little pocket-size portable telephones, some of which are already appearing on the market. (Perhaps someday we'll see a Dick Tracy wristwatch/two-way telephone.)

The FCC hasn't yet decided how to award these licenses, but taxpayers beware. If history is any precedent, they are already shaping another massive giveaway of *our* airwaves.

Where do we apply?

22

FEDERAL EMPLOYEES, BENEFITS

Nice Work If You Can Get It

THERE WAS a time when working for Uncle Sam guaranteed low pay and reasonable benefits.

Things have changed. Federal employment now beats the typical private-sector job in virtually any category you can imagine, especially in benefits that are no longer just "fringe." Working with their friends in Congress and the White House, the Washington bureaucracy has created as close to a heaven-on-the-job as you can get.

The laundry list of benefits is long, and naturally, it's all at the expense of the burdened, insecure taxpayer.

Everyone deserves good health insurance. Washington may not care about the 37 million people without it, or self-employed people who pay too much, or those virtually excluded for health reasons. But it takes good care of its own.

The government pays out $8 billion a year for health coverage for its 4 million civilian employees and retirees and their dependents. Employees have a choice of plans. The government picks up the bulk (68%) of the cost. There is no medical exam, no waiting for pre-existing conditions, and the worker cannot be dropped or have his premium raised no matter how sick he is. (Legislation to do the same for regular citizens has never gotten through Congress.)

The typical policy costs the employee less than $1000 a year for self and family.

Not only does the plan cover employees, but the government continues the coverage and its subsidy for retirees. Most leave government service at age fifty-five, and stay on the plan until they get Medicare. The taxpayer bill for just the retirees is enormous—$3.519 billion a year and growing.

Federal employees beat the general public in vacation time as well. They start with 2.6 weeks, then escalate to 3.9 weeks after 3 years. Finally, it reaches 5.2 weeks after 15 years. *Plus*, they receive 2.6 weeks sick leave as soon as they start, time that can also be used for vacation. So a senior worker gets 2 months off a year with full pay.

What if a federal employee becomes disabled through no fault of the government? If he cannot work, for any reason, he receives early retirement for the rest of his life, even if he's only twenty-five.

There's cheap life insurance as well. Based on salary, it's subsidized and continues into retirement. A thirty-four-year-old employee who makes $40,000 a year can receive $83,000 coverage for only $17 a month. As his salary rises, so does the coverage.

The generous government funded by you and me has always paid for the tuition when an employee took a "work-related" college course or two. But in 1990, buried as an amendment in a Defense Authorization Act, a new free-college plan was born that will cost taxpayers a fortune.

All federal workers, regardless of their work or career goals, can now enroll in college for a bachelor's degree, go on for a master's degree, then even complete a Ph.D.— and Uncle Sam will pick up the full tab!

The rewards of government employment are rich, but the costs are becoming too burdensome for the rest of us. **Something has to be cut back. Here are some logical choices:**

(1) Reduce the 2.6 week vacation time to 2 weeks for employees with less than 3 years on the job. Do not jump to 3 weeks until 5 years, then keep that as the maximum.

(2) Do not permit unspent sick leave to be used as vacation time.

(3) Increase employee contribution to health plans from 32% to 50%.

(4) Increase employee contribution to their life-insurance premiums.

(5) Repeal the freebie college plan. There's no evidence that more schooling will make the well-educated bureaucracy more efficient.

(6) Discontinue government support for retiree health insurance. They are well pensioned (see PENSIONS, FEDERAL EMPLOYEES), and between retirement and the time they go on Medicare, they can pay the premiums themselves.

How much will be saved? Probably $10 billion a year, or more.

The deficit will be smaller and the benefit-happy federal worker will still survive, even flourish, in the warm Washington environment.

23

FERTILIZER

It Doesn't Grow Money

FERTILIZER? What could Uncle Sam have to do with that?

Plenty. For some 60 years he's been in the business of manufacturing it, at an enormous cost with no rewards of significance.

Like so many activities in which Washington is involved, this had historic origins, then just continued on, partially because the legislature and the President forgot about it. But they also forgot that it cost the taxpayers some $30 million a year.

The factory, called the National Fertilizer Development Center, is located near Muscle Shoals, Alabama, and is part of the TVA. The plant was designed to produce nitrates for use in munitions during World War I, but the war ended abruptly before it could be used. Between 1918 and 1933, the factory just sat there, then was converted to fertilizer production during the New Deal, turning out nitrogen and phosphates for farm use.

During its heyday, the plant made a few hundred thousand tons of fertilizer a year, sold it to co-ops and TVA customers, and gave it away to universities. It also marketed the fertilizer to "mixers," companies that added it to their own blend, sold under many names.

The government was never a large factor in the fertilizer world, producing much less than 1% of the nation's total. About three years ago, production was further scaled back to 12,000 tons, the emphasis changed to "research," and the costs cut down toward $20 million a year. But the federal fertilizer factory still operates eight field offices throughout the country, with salesmen making door-to-door calls to peddle Uncle Sam's product in competition with private industry.

The Office of Management and Budget has recommended closing down Washington's fertilizer business, but Muscle Shoals continues to churn out the nitrogen and phosphates, whether anybody wants them or not.

The solution is simple:

For once, the OMB is right. Shut it down and save the $20 million budget. Or sell it and pocket the cash. Money doesn't grow on trees, fertilized or not.

24

FOOD STAMPS

Let's Make a Deal

A HOME BUYER liked a small house he saw, but he had an unusual request. He asked to pay for it with food stamps, which is, of course, illegal. The government-issued scrip can be used only to buy groceries at authorized stores. But the real-estate broker, who obviously knew how to change the stamps into cash in the underground trade, agreed. The buyer paid $1000 in stamps as a down payment, then got the keys to the house when he delivered the remaining $29,000 in food stamps.

Unfortunately for the broker, the "buyer" was an agent of the Inspector General's Office of the Department of Agriculture. The real-estate broker was sentenced to eight months in jail.

Trafficking in food stamps, which generally brings 50 cents on the dollar in volume, is becoming a giant business in America, as some people would rather take the cash than buy food for their children. This waste of federal funds is hard to estimate, but some place all fraud in food stamps at almost $2 billion a year.

The expansion of the food stamp program has been phenomenal in the last decade, eliminating any sound reason for hunger in America. In addition to such welfare programs as Aid to Families with Dependent Children (which provides cash subsidies) and rent vouchers that allow a poor family to live alongside working-class people in apartment houses, food stamps are the third leg of the government's welfare program.

In 1992, 25 million Americans were enrolled in the program at some time of the year, at a cost to the Treasury of $22 billion.

Food stamps come in $1, $5, and $10 denominations, and the allowances are probably higher than most middle-class people believe. A welfare family of four receives $370 in food stamps a month, about $90 a week, more than some employed families can afford to spend for food. The program is actually open to working families with incomes up to about $22,000, but benefits decrease considerably the closer you get to that maximum.

One great problem with the program is that the stamps are too much like currency, and swindles in the millions are commonplace. Twenty-two people in Texas were recently charged with using food stamps to buy cocaine from dealers. In Albany, New York, workers in grocery stores were arrested for exchanging food stamps for narcotics and cash and six have pled guilty. In New Jersey, owners of a retail store bought $149,000 in food stamps for $75,000 in cash. They had become food stamp "fences," cashing in the stamps to the government for the full amount. They have since pled guilty.

Since food stamps cannot be used to buy such items as beer and cigarettes the temptation is increased for people to sell their stamps in the underground market for as little as 30–40 cents on the dollar.

The government is aware of the problem. Puerto Rico, a heavy user of stamps, has decided to relax the rules, and instead of stamps, gives clients the food allowance directly in cash.

On the mainland, experiments are going on to stem the tide of fraud by using "credit cards" instead of food stamps. In several cities, including Minneapolis, Minnesota; Reading, Pennsylvania; Baltimore, Maryland; and Albuquerque, New Mexico, the recipients receive a card that goes through a computer at the grocery store, which deducts the purchase from the person's authorized amount.

"There are a few loopholes in the new system," says a government auditor. "The customer can still make a deal with the grocery-store manager and—instead of groceries—get half the amount in cash. Meanwhile, the store rings up the full purchase. But overall, we think it's cutting down the cheating a lot."

What can be done to stem the fraud? More important, what can be done to reduce the $22 billion, and growing, cost of the whole food stamp program?

First, the credit card system will eliminate most, if not all, the trafficking in stamps, which is getting out of hand.

But perhaps the best thing we can do as a nation is to get rid of the deficit. Once that's done, the economy will blossom and fewer people will need Uncle Sam's largesse to put food on their table.

25

FOREST SERVICE

How to Lose Money in the Timber Business

A LARGE PRIVATE WOOD-PRODUCTS COMPANY came upon a parcel of land in the Rocky Mountains and arranged to cut down an enormous acreage of trees. When they were finished, they hauled off the lumber and sent a check to the landlord.

Who was the owner? The U.S. Forest Service, which has more timber land in the United States than all the private firms combined, and then some.

The agency owns—on behalf of the government—191 million acres of forests, or 12% of the entire land mass of the United States, an area larger than the states of Texas and Montana combined.

In 1935, when holdings were about the same size as now, that vast preserve was handled by 4000 Forest Service employees. Today, that roster has mushroomed beyond recognition into a legion of 33,000 people.

Unlike other federal agencies, the Forest Service brings in money, but as in the Rocky Mountain area, just not enough. It sells an enormous amount of timber each year—8.5 billion board feet in 1991—but it's never enough to turn a profit. When they are finished with their inflated expenses, they're selling the nation's natural resources at below cost, a situation that is getting worse all the time.

Unlike private timber companies who would go broke, the Forest Service's costs are rising four times faster than their income, and more rapidly than they can sell wood.

In 1986, they took in $1.3 billion from timber sales and spent $2 billion, a deficit of $700 million. By 1990, their budget had grown to $3.6 billion, while their receipts had barely increased to $1.7 billion. The Forest Service now runs a yearly deficit of almost $2 billion, a trend leading to fiscal oblivion.

There are many reasons for this, including mismanagement, payments to states, and the use of certain unproductive areas within their network of 119 forests. But one major reason is that the Forest Service has played Santa Claus to the wealthy wood-products companies that buy and cut their trees. The gift of taxpayer funds comes in the form of roads built by the government throughout the timber areas—a network longer than the entire interstate highway system combined—so that industry can have easy access for their logging.

The cost of the road giveaway to date? Several billions that should have stayed in the federal Treasury. And there's also a continuing expense of over $200 million a year for new timber roads.

What's the solution?

(1) Appreciably cut back the manpower of the Forest Service.

(2) Tell the wood-products companies to build their own roads if they want the taxpayers' timber. Or else compensate the government.

(3) Find out which forests are unprofitable and close them to logging.

Meanwhile, where does a citizen sign up to buy government lumber wholesale?

26

FORMER CONGRESSMEN

The Super-Lobbyists

A SMALL CROWD gathered in the Capitol's marble hall outside the House of Representatives trying to gain the attention of members on their way in.

These were not curious tourists. They were lobbyists, part of the mob of 6200 registered with the House Clerk, whose field troops spend hours each day talking, cajoling, even intimidating Representatives to influence them on everything from farm subsidies to tax legislation.

The Congressmen walked onto the House floor while a doorkeeper—who recognized every member on sight—made sure the lobbyists held their place. But suddenly three of the crowd flashed special ID cards with photos. Without a hassle, they followed the Congressmen into the hallowed chamber, where our hard-earned trillions were blithely being spent.

Who were these privileged lobbyists?

They were *former Congressmen*, who, for the rest of their natural lives, retain the privilege of walking onto the House floor at all times, even in the middle of votes that could mean money in the bank for their clients. Once there, they're not supposed to lobby, but that restriction defies definition, even from the best Jesuitical mind. The former members of the Senate have the same privilege in *both* Houses of Congress.

"Altogether, there have been 11,000 members of Congress. We believe there are 800 alive, and about 600 belong to our organization," says the head of the U.S. Association of Former Members of Congress, who is himself a lobbyist.

Where are they now? Not surprisingly, a lot live in the Washington, D.C., area, the scene of their one-time heyday. After a few terms as Congressmen, it's hard to get them back on the farm.

Washington, with its cultural and financial charms, offers great opportunity for a retired or defeated Congressman to cash in on his experience. As a lobbyist he can easily earn two or even three times as much as he did when still on the job. And no longer will he have to suffer microscopic scrutiny; he can enjoy his enlarged bank account in sublime privacy.

Armed with status and access to his former buddies, even in the House or Senate Cloakroom, Dining Room, Gym, or Swimming Pool, he can *finally* accomplish legislative miracles—if not for the public, at least for the piper who pays for the tune.

How many ex-Congressmen are now toiling in the vineyards of special interest, to mix another metaphor?

"It's hard to say exactly," answers an editor of a specialty newspaper that covers Congress, "but there are a lot. I'd guess maybe half of them become lobbyists. Check it with the House Clerk where they have to register."

Not surprisingly, that proved fruitless. "We don't keep records that way. We have no way of knowing how many of the registered lobbyists are former Congressmen," said a spokesperson for the Clerk.

Perpetual floor privileges are not their only reward. Former Congressmen receive pensions (the only federal employees who get retirement pay after only five years' service); they can attend the State of the Union speeches; they can park in Congress's underground garages, free of charge; and use most House and Senate facilities, including the gym and tennis courts, on the same terms as present Congressmen.

So where's the big waste?

It's not in the few dollars that costs the government. The problem is that these former legislators are really good at their new jobs. The overblown federal budget has evolved mainly as the result of special-interest pleadings. With new *super-lobbyists* on the scene after each term, we can expect still more billions to be drained from the depleted Treasury.

What's the answer? Simple.

Former White House employees are not permitted to lobby the Executive Branch for a period. Congress should pass similar legislation covering their own members, prohibiting them from lobbying for five years after they leave office. The floor privilege, or abuse, should be immediately stricken from the books.

This will bring most of them back to where they belong—home with the rest of us—and out of harm's way.

27

FORMER PRESIDENTS

Broke No More

THIS IS a tough one.

In the old days, some Presidents left office broke and even died in modest or poor circumstances, as happened to Ulysses S. Grant. Harry Truman went back to Independence without a presidential pension, which many citizens felt was an outrage.

That situation has now been rectified—with a vengeance.

In 1958, Congress set up a whole system of near-Presidential perks for former Presidents, one that is still in force. It has put them in a supra-class of retired politicians, one that exists nowhere else in the democratic world. But it is consistent with our current view of political leaders as near-royalty.

What do they get? First, a very handsome pension. Gerald Ford, who served only two years in the Oval Office, receives—as do all former Chief Executives—$148,300 a year for the rest of his life. The pension is taxable, but it goes up each year with the cost of living.

There's a kind of regal aspect to their political after-life. The government pays for an office, a staff, telephone, postage, supplies, travel, printing, equipment, utilities, and so on. If we look at the 1993 requested budget, we see that there's inequality among ex-Presidents in what they want and get from the Office of Former Presidents, run by the General Services Administration.

President Reagan's rent in downtown LA is $345,000 a year, almost five times higher than Jimmy Carter's. But Jimmy is number one in printing—$28,000—equipment rentals, telephone, and postage. The travel leaders are Reagan and Ford—$46,000—while Carter's travel budget is virtually non-existent. Nixon's costs are about average in all respects. The fifth person in the system is Lady Bird Johnson, who receives $20,000 a year, plus some postage money.

The total cost of the retire-in-style program is not enormous—$2.2 million a year. The judgment to be made is not monetary, but rather whether it is, or is not, suitable for ex-Presidents to receive such taxpayer attention and assistance now that things have changed radically since the dark days of Ulysses S. Grant.

Today, ex-Presidents almost automatically sign multi-million-dollar contracts for autobiographies, and receive upwards of $50,000 for a single speech, a skill at which President Ford is reportedly expert. They are all, by any definition, rich men.

The $2 million federal subsidy is only the beginning. Two other post-White House expenses are much more costly. Each former President and his wife (or President's widow) receive Secret Service protection against cranks and worse for the rest of their lives, as do their children up to age sixteen. President Nixon has dismissed his, which has reportedly produced a saving of $3 million a year. But the recent near-attack on President Reagan by an anti-nuke protestor shows there's something to be said for that expenditure.

There's much less justification for our modern obsession with Presidential libraries. Most people believe these are nonprofit private enterprises. It's true that they were mainly built with private contributions, but the taxpayer then takes over and pays to run them. Forever.

There are *nine* Presidential libraries on the federal payroll. Three involve living Presidents—Carter, Ford, and Reagan—but six are now history: Hoover, FDR, Truman, Eisenhower, Kennedy, and Johnson.

What about Nixon? He has a library out in Yorba Linda, California, but, surprisingly, the government does not pay for its upkeep. Why?

"In 1974, the Congress passed legislation that says that the Nixon papers had to be kept within the Washington, D.C., area," says a spokesperson for the National Archives, which administers the program. "So we have a special section here that holds them. Therefore, the government doesn't pay for the upkeep of the Nixon library in California."

The cost of maintaining the Presidential library system and its 249-member staff has now reached $25 million a year. In addition, the government pays for most renovations and alterations. Millions have already been spent, and Congress has authorized $8.5 million to fix up the JFK Library in Boston and $5 million for the Hoover operation.

The personal upkeep of the former Presidents is not something that's open-ended. No matter how much we wish them well and pamper them, they are mortal.

But the Presidential library program has all the makings of a future federal albatross. As each new ex-President joins the rolls, ad infinitum, it means another library. With upkeep, expansion, renovations, inflation, et cetera, it won't be long before we're looking at a $100

million tab, an increasingly common figure for supposedly small federal sub-agencies.

What can we do?

This is probably the right time to scale back our historical intentions. First, we should *not* pay for any capital
improvements in the libraries as we're now doing. The
nonprofit institutions that built them have demonstrated
their ability to raise money. Second, we should scale back
federal support of their operations over a period of years,
until they are totally *self-supporting* through donations
and entrance and research fees.

With the weight of our enormous deficit, we can
scarcely afford the luxury of an endless string of taxpayer-
financed Presidential libraries.

We love or hate them in office, then we pamper them
in retirement. But that doesn't mean we have to pick up
the tab for their infinite after-life.

28

FORMER SPEAKERS

Enough Already

THERE ARE three living former Speakers of the House of Representatives—Carl Albert of Oklahoma, Jim Wright of Texas, and Thomas "Tip" O'Neill of Massachusetts.

The last two were especially colorful political characters, and despite controversy, some people were sorry to see them go. Well, their fans, whoever they are, don't have to worry, and their many enemies have been foiled.

They're no longer members of Congress, but, courtesy of the U.S. taxpayer, they haven't left us at all. Not for a minute. In fact, they cost us three times as much out of office as they did when they were running the House.

No, this is not because of their extravagant federal pensions.

If you'll check the report of the Clerk of the House—which I've done—you'll learn that there is an Office of Former Speakers. It's an elaborate and expensive set-up to take care of these one-time public servants in the gilded manner they had gotten used to. (See CONGRESS, LEADERS.)

This is not some short transition period to ease the shock of loss of power. The Office of Former Speakers shelters them for the rest of their natural lives, at taxpayer expense.

The existence of this golden parachute seems to be a dark secret in Washington.

"May I speak with Mr. So-and-So?" I asked the Capitol phone operator, giving the name of a former Speaker's aide I had plucked out of the Clerk's report.

"Never heard of him," she said after checking her directory.

"But he's listed as a government employee, he's part of the Office of Former Speakers, and he gets paid $60,000 a year according to the book," I said rapidly. "Only I don't know exactly for what."

"I never heard of the Office of Former Speakers, and I've been here twenty years," she responded haughtily. "Are you sure you know what you're talking about?"

After I read her the item from the report, on page 47, she switched me to personnel.

"Yes, we do have that gentleman on our list, but I don't know where he works, and from what I can see he has no phone."

I tried several other offices on the Hill, without luck, then decided to try the present Speaker's office.

"No, I never heard of this person or the Office of Former Speakers," he said, then suggested I call one of the "formers" myself. He gave me the phone number for Jim Wright in Fort Worth, Texas.

I called, and sure enough I had reached one of the three offices of the Office of Former Speakers.

Each "former" gets a staff of three people, including an administrative assistant, who can be paid as much as $96,000 a year, plus two secretaries, plus $67,000 a year for his office upkeep. This runs the federal government about $700,000 annually, a cost that goes on until they all die. In broad brush strokes, that means about $15 million the taxpayers will pay for the privilege of—what?

But this is only the beginning. Talk is circulating that Speaker Foley may leave after only three years on the job, which will add another $5 million to the "former" overhead. And who's to say the roster of one-time Speakers could not reach five, or six, or ten?

The rationale, like much in Washington, is hard to comprehend outside the Beltway. Why should former Speakers be treated as ex-royalty, memorialized in office, with staffs and official digs, forever, just as if they never voluntarily left, or were perhaps thrown out by their colleagues, or the voters? What about ex-Vice Presidents? And ex-Chairmen of Committees? And ex-Cabinet officers?

Are we never to get rid of our politicians once we elect them? Is there no mercy in this land for the beleaguered taxpayer?

Everyone, of course, knows the answer to that rhetorical question.

29

GOVERNMENT DEFICIT AND DEBT

The Double Whammy

IN 1985, three courageous, if foolhardy, Congressmen pushed through a bill that everyone thought augured well for the future of the country.

Finally, someone was about to do something to curb the enormous debt and deficit. It was the Gramm-Rudman-Hollings Bill, which was passed by Congress and signed by the President. Everyone confidently believed it would eliminate the deficit by 1991, and thus hold the debt below the $3 trillion mark.

Well, we're now past that deadline. What has happened?

First, Senator Warren Rudman of New Hampshire, one of the authors of the bill, has quit Congress in disgust. Second, the federal debt has passed $4 trillion and is on its way to at least $6 trillion by the end of the decade. The promised "zero" deficit of 1991 has reached $400 billion in 1992.

The hope of reduced deficits leading to a balanced budget has vanished with the dream. Not only does the deficit (annual) and public debt (cumulative) rise each year, but the White House's Office of Management and Budget—a sophist title if ever there was one—keeps underestimating it with the same fervor with which the deficit increases.

In the fiscal 1992 budget, the OMB predicted that the deficit would be $281 billion. By 1996, it boasted, it would vanish entirely. In its place, the OMB claimed, the nation would then have a *surplus* of $20 billion.

As a resident of the worn-down Lower East Side of New York once answered former Governor Nelson Rockefeller as his hand swept majestically across the vision of a new city that would supposedly sprout there: "You should live so long."

What has actually happened in just one year?

The OMB's deficit estimate for 1992 has already been upped 40% to $399.7 billion (they cleverly shy away from the $400 billion number). The fantasy of a surplus in 1996 has now turned, pumpkinlike, into a $183 billion deficit estimate for that same year, surely another OMB delusion.

Why is the deficit so important?

First, it is a swift moving item not under any control. An electronic sign in Midtown Manhattan keeps us informed on the current national debt, which rises three quarters of a million dollars a minute. The Bureau of the Public Debt (yes, there is one) sends out a daily fact sheet with scores of statistics chronicling our financial misery.

Most important, the government deficit forces the Treasury into the credit market to borrow enormous sums on a continual basis. This pushes up interest rates for the nation as a whole—whether for mortgages, car loans, or corporate financing. As Washington sells Treasury bills and bonds backed by the "full credit" of the United States, they encourage higher rates on the long-term 30-year bond, which is at the core of most interest calculations.

Back in 1950, when the nation was fiscally strong, the total national debt was only $256 billion, most of it accumulated during World War II. The long bond was a mere 2.4% (!) and home mortgages were between 4% and 5%, about half of today's level. Naturally, there was an unprecedented building boom, in which homeowners could finance the then-typical $10,000 mortgage for $50 a month. In 1960, when the deficit had barely risen to $290 billion, the long bond was only 4.9%.

Even by 1970, the nation was still relatively healthy. The federal debt was $380.9 billion, actually less in constant dollars than in 1950. But it was during the seventies and eighties—the liberal Carter and conservative Reagan and Bush administrations—that the deficit, the debt, and the T-bond exploded in our faces.

By the end of the 1970s, the debt had reached almost a trillion dollars and the T-bond stood at a stifling 10–12%. Today, the public debt has more than quadrupled. Though the T-bond has come down somewhat, it is still historically very high.

The debt is a double-barreled whammy. Not only does it keep the long bond up, but because the government is constantly borrowing new money, the annual interest carrying charges regularly rise as well. In 1993, with an expected $348 billion deficit, we will be paying $315 billion in interest just to carry the debt.

The debt and deficit create a joint spiral, finally leading to fiscal oblivion.

What can we do? It's not so simple, but quite possible:

(1) Eliminate the deficit by making $400 billion in cuts from the annual budget, a task which is not as difficult as it seems. (Read *The Government Racket*.)

(2) Having done that, we can start to control the $300-billion-plus interest carrying charge on the debt. Since the elimination of the deficit will force the long bond to tumble—perhaps to as low as 5%—we can refinance the

debt (whose paper turns over every six years) at much lower interest rates. The savings will be at least $100 billion a year.

(3) The final step will be to eliminate the public debt entirely by amortizing it, like a mortgage, over a 40-year period. If we could *begin* to accomplish this, the boom in a renovated America would surprise even the headiest optimists.

But for this to become a reality, we would need to find leaders of enormous political strength and courage.

Here, you're strictly on your own.

30

HELIUM

Way Up in the Air

HELIUM, like in gas bags? Absolutely.

The American government is in the helium business in a large way. And as is traditional in federal programs, it's been a fiscal disaster.

Washington so loves helium that it has a *billion* dollars worth of gas stored underground in the Texas panhandle for fear it will run out of the inert gas. While the gas sits, the Bureau of Mines of the Department of Interior suffers a loss of $100 million a year.

"How much helium do we have underground?" I asked a director of the program in Washington.

At least he was frank. "We have a whole lot—in fact, 35 billion cubic feet."

"How long will that last at our present rate of use?" I asked innocently.

He didn't hesitate. "Well over a hundred years."

A century? How did this gaseous state of irrationality evolve?

Actually, it's a tragic bureaucratic story. It all started with blimps in World War I. Military strategists decided the airships were the weapon of the future, and in 1929, Congress appropriated money to put the government into the helium-producing business in case we had to fight that war all over again.

Plants were built and for 30 years, the U.S. government was the major (almost exclusive) producer of helium in the United States. Washington provided all the helium needed by agencies like NASA—who used it to purge fuel tanks in the missile program—then sold the rest to private industry.

In 1960, Congress decided to escalate helium production and hoard most of it for future needs. The plan was to store an enormous amount, about 4 billion cubic feet a year, some ten times what was actually used.

The Bureau of Mines contracted with private industry to build five refining plants. The government agreed to buy the output for $138 million. They did, but to get the money, the Bureau had to raise the price of helium (which, incidentally, is extracted from natural gas) from $15 to $35 for 1000 cubic feet.

This was Washington's undoing. The higher price made it profitable for private industry to get in the picture. Soon companies like Exxon were outproducing the government, and supplying new needs like MRI diagnostic machines, underwater welding, and some laser uses. While private firms were selling helium and making a profit, the Bureau was squirreling it underground for the twenty-second century. And going deeper and deeper into debt.

In the end, the helium operation of the U.S. government ended up with four eggs on its bureaucratic face:

(1) Private industry has pushed so far ahead that it, not the government, now controls 90% of the business. (2) The U.S. government helium operation is in debt $1.2 billion. (3) Washington is stuck with most of the world's helium supply, which can't be used up until the year 2101. Should the government try to dump it on the market, the price would be driven down to zilch. (4) We lose

$100 million a year in interest on the loan taken out to fill that big hole under Texas.

The solution?

Sell the installation and pipeline in Texas to private industry and get out of the helium business entirely. Sell off the stockpile a little at a time so as not to ruin the price. And the next time the U.S. government announces that it intends to corner the market on any commodity, run for the fiscal hills!

By the way, what ever happened to the blimps that started it all?

31

HIGHWAYS AND ROADS

Making Deals on the Interstate

THE THREE-MILE-LONG Suspended Light Rail System Technology Pilot Project is not only a classic government title, it's a $35 million monorail that is being built by the federal government as part of the $153 billion Intermodal Surface Transportation Efficiency Act of 1991.

The project is one of thousands that will come out of this bill, financed by an extra 5 cents gasoline tax approved during the 1990 budget deal, on top of the 9 cents before that.

What's so special about the Disneyesque monorail? Nothing much, except that by a non-coincidence it was awarded to a part of the nation that needs it as much as it needs a crocodile-infested theme park. The monorail had been projected for a small town in Pennsylvania—specifically, Altoona—population 57,000.

The Chairman of the Subcommittee on Surface Transportation is Congressman Bud Shuster of Pennsylvania. His district? Where else but Altoona.

But angry outcries forced a change in plans. The site of the futuristic train will be chosen in "a national competition," as a Congressional spokesman explained.

This was only one of 460 "demonstration projects" attached to the mammoth bill. Congressman Shuster managed to put in 13 projects worth $287 million for his own district. In all, these "demo" items will cost the taxpayers $6.8 *billion*.

The highway system, which includes the completed interstate network, has been one of the few government successes in the last 30 years. Therefore, it's disheartening to see it marred so badly by Congressmen.

"All roads, you know, are state and local roads, even if they have the U.S. label, like U.S. 1. The interstate is just made up of connecting state roads," explains an auditor who handles government highway matters. "But in deciding how the federal money from 'Iced Tea'—that's our name for the large Intermodal Transportation bill—should be spent, the Federal Highway Administration and the state people consult, using specific guidelines on what should be done. But when Congressmen want projects for their own district, they just earmark them right in the law, and it goes over the top. There's no screening and they don't have to meet state criteria. And many of the projects don't."

The money for these roads comes almost exclusively from our gasoline taxes, which go into the Highway Trust Fund. But here again, Washington disappoints us.

"There is about an $11 billion surplus in the fund from unspent gasoline taxes," explains a Federal Highway Administration official. "But the money has been borrowed by the Treasury."

"Trust fund" money has been borrowed? As we shall see in an even larger item, this is a Washington habit. By co-mingling trust and general receipts, the government can—and does—make the deficit seem smaller than it is.

What should be done to keep everyone's fingers out of the highway pie?

(1) First, the trust fund should be segregated. We didn't increase our gas taxes to feed the deficit.

(2) Second, $6 billion is real money. Congress should pass a law restricting its own members from adding projects that don't go through normal Highway Administration and state road channels.

It's bad enough our gas taxes keep going up. But does that mean we need "demonstration projects" that only demonstrate how politically greedy our Congressmen have become?

32

HONEY

Sweets for the Beekeepers

WHO DOESN'T like honey?

The federal government apparently loves it, for over the last decade it has bought and stored hundreds of millions of pounds of honey that had been surrendered by beekeepers cashing in their unpaid federal loans.

But critics fear that Washington has been badly stung.

"In 1985, we reported to Congress that the program for commercial beekeepers was too expensive and probably unneeded," says a General Accounting Office spokesman. "We recommended closing it down. At first it looked like Congress would go along, then suddenly they changed their mind. Instead, they actually increased subsidies for beekeepers. I suppose our report brought it to their attention."

The honey lobby, like those of most farm commodities, is alive and buzzing despite critics. The debacle that prompted the report came in 1983 when just a few thousand honey farmers handed the government half their crop for cash. They received more money from Washington—who had to store, then give the honey away free—than they would have by selling it in the marketplace.

Not only did it cost the government a fortune to

acquire the unwanted honey, but as a result the American market dried up. The public had to buy *imported* honey while the Department of Agriculture warehouses were filled with our own product! In fact, the 110 million pounds of honey imported that year was exactly equal to the amount the U.S. was squirreling away.

This exasperating program has cost nearly a billion dollars to date. In 1980–83 alone, the subsidy and storage costs ran to $164 million.

How did it all begin? Like many federal programs, this one had an earlier purpose that has long since vanished. The beekeeping industry expanded during World War II when honey was used as a sugar substitute, and beeswax served to waterproof ammunition. But after the war, beekeepers were stuck with a surplus of honey and a shortage of customers. In an American tradition, they turned to the government, and the honey subsidy was born.

Did the 1983 debacle cure Congress of laying out fortunes to a handful of recipients? (Only a few thousand beekeepers got the whole hive of money.)

Far from it. The program is richer than ever before. A beekeeper can now borrow money from the government at the rate of 54 cents a pound of honey collateral. He pays no interest on the loan, and can repay the money after the crop season, at the rate of only 49 cents. So even if it all goes well and he markets his honey crop, he makes a profit of 5 cents a pound on just his government loan!

Has this gift spared the government from having to buy his honey and give it away?

Hardly.

"In 1988, we had to take in 32 million pounds of honey from beekeepers," says a Department of Agriculture official. "The industry had a bumper crop, so prices dropped and the subsidy clicked in. It cost us about $100 million that year. In 1990 we were luckier. We had to pay out only $18 million."

Has Congress tried to close down the expensive program?

"They passed a law saying a beekeeper could only pledge 250,000 pounds of honey. [That would mean a $130,000 subsidy per bee farmer]," says the Aggie spokesperson. "But the honey producers lobbied and Congress took off the restriction."

What can be done?

There's no doubt that the entire program should be closed down immediately. "There's no reason to support it," says a GAO spokesman. "Most payments go to a few people, and they're mainly big companies."

But the farm lobby and some in the Department of Agriculture disagree. They claim bees are needed not only for the honey, but for pollinating plants and fruit trees.

On the other hand, the GAO is convinced that beekeepers, some of whom already offer commercial pollination services, would merely shift their emphasis. "The program is unnecessary to ensure pollination," confidently states a report.

So the next time you spread honey on your bread, or put it in your cake mix, think nostalgically of the beekeeper.

He's not only getting paid for keeping his honey out of the market. He's making a fat profit just by taking out interest-free federal loans on his bees.

What could be sweeter?

33

INDIANS

Back on the Reservation

THAT THERE ARE a million Native Americans living on or near hundreds of Indian reservations, mainly in the West, is probably known to most. What is not known is the enormous amount of federal money being spent, much of it wastefully, to try to improve their conditions.

We immigrants took their land, starting in 1630 in New England, until all of it was conquered by the end of the nineteenth century, despite Sitting Bull's valiant last-ditch attempt to stem the Anglo tide.

In 1992, the Bureau of Indian Affairs spent $1.7 billion, or about $1700 on each Indian in the 507 federally recognized tribes. But this is only the beginning of our financial involvement with those who once owned the country.

A computer printout requested by this writer from the Office of Management and Budget shows that the total amount appropriated by thirteen different agencies in 1991 was actually *$4.7 billion*, or almost $5000 for each reservation Indian, the only ones for whom the government has special programs. (The other million Indians live in the American mainstream and receive no aid.)

To put it another way, the U.S. Treasury spends *$20,000* on each Indian family of four.

The Indian budgets vary from $1.9 billion from Health

and Human Services to $1.7 billion from Interior (the Bureau of Indian Affairs) to $517 million from Education and $123 million from Agriculture. Even Commerce spent $4 million on the reservations.

Has this enormous amount accomplished an equal amount of good?

Few think so. Many reservation Indians live in near-abject poverty, with an unemployment rate of 45%. Although there is widespread diabetes and alcoholism, the general health record has improved. The birth rate is quite high and infant mortality has, for the most part, been conquered. The tribes run 21 community colleges, and there are a few four-year-degree institutions as well. Most Indian children (85%) attend regular public schools, and the others learn in special schools run by the BIA.

But the situation is still shameful overall. Too many Indians, like the Sioux tribes in Dakota, live in great, unrelieved poverty.

Of course, some tribes do better than others. The Cherokees in Oklahoma are famous for their relative success and integration. Thirty reservations across the nation now sponsor gaming casinos (a sign of Indian "governmental" rights), and others have attracted light industry.

The status of the American Indian is peculiar and special. Indians have been American citizens since 1924. They vote and pay federal taxes (when they earn enough) like everyone else, and serve in the armed forces. But the reservation has certain "extraterritorial" rights. Several Presidents, including the last half dozen, have verified that the relationship of the U.S. government to the tribes is one of "government to government."

The exaggeration is typical of Washington, but the Indians do have limited local powers, including exclusion from state taxes on money earned on the reservations, and certain tribal prerogatives.

Some of the reservation lands are quite large. The Navajo home in Arizona and surrounding states is larger than all of West Virginia. Indian land is owned in three ways: outright by the tribes; by a number of tribespeople collectively; or by individual Indians. Washington likes to deny that American Indians are wards of the state, but Indians cannot buy or sell their land without permission of the Department of Interior. The land is supposedly "held in trust" for them by the U.S. government, which was once mockingly called "The Great White Father."

No one is happy with the state of Indian affairs, yet no one seems to know what to do about it, except to throw $5 billion at the problem each year.

In the 1950s, the government decided to break, or "terminate," its special relations with the Indians and treat them like any other citizens. But that failed, and since then, the relationship has been one of partial paternalism. The heads of the BIA are generally Native Americans and most of the BIA staff are Indian, which is officially defined as having at least one-fourth Indian blood. To verify the claim, the BIA has even developed an elaborate genealogical chart.

So what's the basic problem? It's a failure of the BIA and Washington, in concert with tribal leaders, to develop a coordinated plan to create a solvent, productive Indian community.

One answer is greater self-rule by the Native American community. In 1975, new laws were passed that would supposedly increase self-determination, but tribal leaders complained that it was not being carried out. In 1991, the General Accounting Office looked into the situation and found that the complaints were accurate.

"Tribal officials told GAO that they were unable to significantly affect budgeting decisions for IPS [Indian Priority System]," says the General Accounting Office. "Tribes expressed particular concern about their lack of participation in formulating budgets."

Today, there are seventeen tribes in a self-governing experiment in which Indians have considerable say over how BIA money will be spent on their reservations. Of course, that's only a third of all federal funds allotted.

What then is a possible fuller answer to the Washington-Indian dilemma?

The federal government should first coordinate its $5 billion spending under a single umbrella, to eliminate all the duplication. Then it should begin a gradual withdrawal from control of the reservations, except for financial support. In place of the present confused relationship, power should be given to the tribes—along with cash.

If the $5 billion, much of which is now wasted, were split among truly self-governing tribal governments and used for the benefit of their people, and not cut up piecemeal by 13 duplicating federal agencies and their bureaucracies, perhaps the Indian community could develop its own resources and greater internal strength.

They could hardly do worse than Washington's waste and mismanagement in the century of stewardship.

And besides, we owe them something better.

34

JOB TRAINING

Big Bucks, Small Bang

JOBS. JOBS. JOBS.

Nothing could be more important, particularly when the economy is soft. The government is aware of the need and spends billions yearly to help train and secure jobs for low-income citizens.

How have they done?

They claim they are doing splendidly. A detailed report from the Department of Labor extolls the efforts of the Joint Training and Partnership Act, sponsored in 1983 by the strange duo of ideological enemies—Dan Quayle and Ted Kennedy. An important part of the government job program, it was set up as a partnership among the federal government, the states, and private industry.

Between October 1983 and June 1991, proudly claims the JTPA, they handled 7 million Americans and placed 4 million in jobs, at a cost of $15.5 billion, or approximately $4000 per position.

Not earth shaking, but not bad either. A half million jobs a year for "disadvantaged" or "economically dislocated" workers won't solve poverty, but it's something for Uncle Sam to be proud of.

But is it true?

"The claims don't mean a thing," frankly states a spokesman at the Inspector General's Office of the Department of Labor. "Four million jobs by whose definition? We have to be very careful about the claims because there are no real federal standards for success or what they mean. One state may call it a job when the person works for two weeks; another could mean a single day; still another may mean that 'successful termination' is filling out a résumé for the applicant."

His cynicism is echoed by an IG report, which states: "According to our audit results, the program is not focusing on hard-to-serve individuals. . . . Additionally, our data shows that the rates of retaining participants in jobs, increasing their earnings, and reducing welfare dependency are not encouraging."

Over the last three years, the IG reports have featured some JTPA horror stories with hints of generalized failure:

• More than 70% of those employed after JTPA training earn less than $5.00 per hour, the type of wages one gets at fast-food chains without any expensive government training.

• 60% of the employers who received subsidies to train workers say they would have hired them without the subsidies.

• In Fort Worth, Texas, the IG found that $441,000 charged to "training" was actually for administrative costs.

• One supposedly "non-profit" JTPA training contractor made $62,000 profit on a $6000 investment.

• A participating Private Industry Council charged JTPA twice the fair-market rent, using the government money to pay off its mortgage.

112

- A Mississippi training contractor made $1.1 million profit, or 23% of the entire contract.
- $2.6 million in training funds went to ineligible workers at the Toyota car factory in Kentucky.
- Almost half the JTPA trainees end up unemployed four months after training.
- In Louisiana, $784,000 given to a local college to train dislocated workers was used to create a television center, which the IG said "was unreasonable, unnecessary, and of no benefit to JTPA."
- In a $38 million training contract in Puerto Rico, all costs under the reimbursable program were charged to training, even though half of it was for administration and other items.
- In a training program in Southern California, JTPA paid out $1.45 million for 800 claimed placements. Actually, 94 were unsupported, and of the remaining 706, each person was reported almost three times. In addition, almost half the work was for three days or less, including placement as movie "extras."

Seventy percent of JTPA money is supposed to go for "training," but one IG spokesman says "the real figure is more like 45%." In one case, the IG's office found only 30% of the funds went to training, with most of the rest to middlemen who brokered the deal.

Other audits of JTPA found the following:

- Too much training time and money were spent on low-skill jobs—like 129 days to "train" a car washer.
- Administrative costs were under-reported, in one case by $456,000.
- Training contractors were overpaid. One received 80% of his full contract funds just by enrolling the people.

• And they questioned the training of those already employed and those who had full work experience in the field. One oil burner technician was "trained" even though he already had five years' experience.

The JTPA program costs taxpayers $4.3 billion a year, but it's only part of the federal government's massive involvement in job training, one of the largest social projects emanating from Washington.

"This year, the government is spending $17 billion in job training and placement of the economically deprived," says an auditor. "There's a lot of confusion, difficulty, and overlap in the government programs. We found 48 different funding flows from 14 different agencies— from Education to Health and Human Services to Labor—with no central intake. Unless the applicant has a road map of the government, it's hard to know what's going on."

One of the best-known programs is the Job Corps, which, with Head Start, is among the last remnants of Lyndon Johnson's War on Poverty.

The Job Corps is the Cadillac of training operations. Approximately 41,000 youngsters from economically disadvantaged homes are housed in more than 100 Job Corps Centers, where they live, study for a high school equivalency diploma, and train for a vocation—from carpentry to auto mechanics.

Some people compare it to FDR's CCC (Civilian Conservation Corps), which operated inexpensively in the woods and was run like a small army.

The Job Corps has residential units in such diverse places as the South Bronx and the wilds of the Rockies. But unlike the CCC, it's not as outdoorsy, and it's *very* expensive. The program spends almost a billion a year for a minuscule number of clients. The cost is $22,000 for each student per annum, about the price of a Harvard University education.

The directors believe the two-year program can make a difference in the lives of its trainees, but 20% are expelled, and the average stay is only eight months. At that price, the same money would provide a full-time job for two beginning workers for a year.

One new program may have merit, if only because it attacks the gnawing problem of those on welfare. Called JOBS and administered by Health and Human Services, it has both a carrot and a stick. It requires welfare mothers with children on AFDC (Aid to Families with Dependent Children) to either enroll in education or training, or seek a job. If they do, they get help with day care for their children. If not, they risk losing one-third of their welfare payments. It costs a billion dollars a year, and it's too early to tell, yet some people have hopes for it.

But there's still $17 billion being spent each year on "job training," from all federal agencies, with increasing proof that too much money is getting much too little for the buck.

What can be done instead to provide jobs for unemployed young men without schooling or training?

The White House has come up with an idea to cut out some of the duplication. It wants to create "Skill Centers," where a person can tap into all the programs in one place. The idea sounds good, but history shows that layers of government bureaucracy—Washington, states, localities, private and public participation—make failure almost inevitable.

What then should be done? Is there a model in our history?

Absolutely. It is Harry Truman's GI Bill of Rights for returning veterans of World War II, which changed the face of America. It included a simple, successful, non-bureaucratic on-the-job training program. It was virtually self-administered and had no eligibility rules or means test. All a veteran had to do was apply for a job that included a skill to be learned—whether as a carpenter, newspaper reporter, draftsman, upholsterer, or whatever.

If the job was approved, as it generally was, the government paid half the veteran's salary for one year, directly to the employer. If the GI stopped working, the subsidy stopped. There was no red tape, no training sessions, no federal interference. In fact, the veteran never saw anyone in the government. The paperwork, which was very minimal, was handled by the employer.

As experience shows, the work environment is the best place to "train," not only in the intricacies of a job, but to pick up needed social skills as well.

How would that work today? Easily. First, it would exclude fast-food jobs. Those are readily available and need no government help. But the others mentioned, and scores more—even learning to run a commercial Xerox machine in a copy shop—would be eligible.

How many jobs could be created?

Take the $17 billion we're now spending. We'll close down all the present government programs, pocket $2 billion to reduce the deficit, and use the remaining $15 billion on the new on-the-job idea. With an entry-level salary of $12,000 a year, Uncle Sam would pay the employer $6000 for each new worker being trained for one year.

Simple arithmetic. Subtract $1 billion for administration, leaving $14 billion. Divide that by $6000. The answer is most encouraging: 2.3 million new jobs a year—almost 12 million in five years, enough to change the face of any deprived community, and get it launched in the direction of work.

Not only is that more jobs than the JTPA ever dreamt of in their bureaucratic visions, but more than the U.S. government has created in all the years since the days of FDR's WPA and Harry Truman's GI Bill.

The social good, the sense of hope, the possibility of real change through *direct* non-bureaucratic action, all seem to make sense.

It's surely a lot better than paying middlemen, contractors, and layers and layers of bureaucracy to *pretend* we're training our dispossessed young people for the real work world.

35

JUNKETS

A $99 Dinner, Please

EVERYONE KNOWS what a junket is: a freebie trip to anywhere enjoyed by corporate brass and others, but not on their own nickel.

The junkets that should disturb us are those charged to Uncle Sam's credit card and then paid for by the taxpayer.

The biggest offenders are politicians—of every party, stripe, and locality. Recently 1700 legislators from all 50 states had a mammoth bash at our expense. The National Conference of State Legislators brought the officials and their spouses and children to—where else?—Orlando, Florida, to confer and visit Disney World.

Everyone got a day on the house. They enjoyed themselves, got in a little talk, and Disney and the hotels made money. All came out ahead, except, of course, the state taxpayers, who picked up the $3 million tab.

(Why are there so few junkets to Cleveland and Buffalo?)

Congressmen are, of course, the champion junketeers of our time. They have business, it seems, everywhere in the world, especially during the nice weather.

Here are a few of the more "necessary" Congressional trips at taxpayer expense:

• A ranking Senator took a delegation of six and their spouses on a twelve-day trip to the Far East, including Singapore, ostensibly to investigate U.S. foreign policy in the area. Cost to the taxpayer, $359,000.

• A House member took an investigative tour of Eastern Europe with several Congressmen and their spouses. Cost? $99,000.

• Nineteen House members toured Israel and Saudi Arabia at a cost of $322,402.

• Five members of the House Committee on Science and Space Technology, along with eleven staffers, made a "vital" trip, which avoided such spots as the Amazon basin but managed to hit such tourist favorites as New Zealand, Australia, and Hong Kong, the mecca of shoppers.

• Twenty-one Congressmen, their spouses, staff, and guests—a total of more than 100 persons—went to the Paris Air Show courtesy of Uncle Sam. Cost? Over $200,000.

I decided to seek help from the Congressional Research Service, part of the Library of Congress. They will aid a citizen if the request is placed through his Congressman. My Representative was pleased to be of service and forwarded the request on Congressional junkets to the CRS.

Two days later I received a call from the Congressman's office.

"I'm sorry, sir, but the Congressional Research Service can't help you," an aide reported. "They have the material, but they can't release any information that mentions specific Congressmen."

So much for small conspiracies.

Not just Congressmen, but bureaucrats, too, are becoming experts at traveling on Uncle Sam's tab. When the Post Office had its recent convention and meeting budget audited, it was found that $6.2 million was spent. But that didn't include travel expenses for these confabs, which ran an additional equal amount. (Many Post Office officials have been found traveling *first class* on commercial airliners.)

Did the Post Office people journey to Detroit or Chicago for their meetings? Hardly.

Four of the audited conferences were held on the island of Maui, Hawaii; in Scottsdale, Arizona; Denver; and Marina del Rey, California. The cost ran as high as $369 per person per day in Scottsdale. Meals alone were $137 per person per day, which included one superb dinner at $99.19 each. Spouses and guests added $27,000 to Uncle Sam's tab.

The junket fever has spread even further, at grave peril to taxpayers. Even firms under contract to Uncle Sam have learned how to have a good time on Uncle Sam's nickel—albeit a large, golden one.

A recent audit of contractors for the Department of Energy showed that the government had been charged $3.5 million for luxury items, including liquor, first-class air tickets, and golf tourney fees.

Two shocking facts emerged. This was an audit of only a few dozen of the more than 1000 contracts handled by the Department. And worse, some of the party-time tab came from firms that operate our nuclear weapons facilities. How does alcohol mix with enriched uranium?

The anti-junket movement has Congress unmoved. Junketing is perhaps its last great perk, and legislators seem to have drawn the line against its erosion. But one Congressman is out to rein in his freely traveling colleagues.

"We've introduced a bill to reform the junket situation," explained a spokesman for Congressman Bob Carr, Democrat of Michigan. "We're asking that before any junket is taken, the committee involved hold a public vote authorizing it. Once the trip is over, the Congressmen would make a statement to the committee reconciling what happened with the authorization."

Good idea? Naturally. But what happened?

"We introduced the bill in November 1990, but it's still stuck in committee," he says.

The whole issue of travel and entertaining is an important one for taxpayers, both in dollar terms and symbolically. Travel is covered later on, but the question of federal employees and contractors billing the government for having a good time is something Washington would rather not face up to.

"How much does the government spend on entertainment?" I asked the Office of Management and Budget.

"Entertainment?" a spokesman responded. "We just don't know. We've never tallied that up."

Perhaps they should.

Solution?

The Carr bill should be recommended out of committee and passed, which will temper Congress's ardor for free travel. An executive order by the President cutting agency meeting and convention budgets in half will also save many millions.

And perhaps *all* such meetings should be held in Washington, D.C., in the hot, humid summertime, which will have little appeal for bureaucrats. That should bring junket costs way down. Hawaii and Scottsdale are too attractive a lure.

As for people on government contracts, all travel and entertainment should be on their nickel, and not ours.

The OMB seems to have the ability to turn out a yearly

2000-page budget with 190,000 separate items, yet is unable to track the entertainment and meeting costs of federal employees and contractors. If they'd like, I'll loan them my antique Apple IIE, and some spread-sheet software. Maybe then they can respond with a figure.

Or is it possible they just don't want to?

36

LAND, PURCHASES

Buy High, Sell Low

THE UNITED STATES GOVERNMENT is obsessed with land.

The federal government is by far the largest land holder in the nation, owning some 700 billion acres, over one-third the total land mass. Government lands are equal in size to all the states west of the Rockies. In fact, Washington owns pieces of every state, ranging as high as 86% of Nevada and 60% of California.

Isn't that enough?

Apparently not. Politicians and bureaucrats, cheered on by special-interest groups, are spending billions in taxpayer dollars to buy up still more land. There is no letup despite the deficit, and one even detects some acceleration.

Four federal agencies are the main players in this modern land grab. The National Forest Service, which already owns a parcel equal to the size of Texas and Wyoming combined, has bought an additional 1.6 million acres, a piece larger than the state of Delaware, at a price of $828 million. Since 1980, the Department of Interior has purchased 177,000 acres, but two other agencies are considerably busier trying to raise Uncle Sam's enormous stockpile of terra firma.

In the last decade, the National Park Service has

bought 250,000 acres at a cost of a half billion dollars and added 88,000 acres by right of condemnation, for which another quarter billion dollars was paid. Half of that went for a most unusual parcel—land *outside* the Civil War Manassas Historic Battlefield in Virginia. The reason? Fear that someone would build a shopping mall near the grounds.

The National Park Service's most recent big buy was the entire 75,000 acre Redwood National Park, a purchase that began in 1968 and ended a decade later. Since the owners didn't want to sell, the Park Service condemned the land by right of eminent domain, which was followed by a fierce court battle. The first parcel cost $200 million, or a reasonable $4000 an acre. But the remainder stuck the taxpayers with an enormous bill. It cost $1.3 *billion*, or almost *$50,000* an acre for raw forest land, surely a national record.

The last of the four land-hungry agencies is the Fish and Wildlife Service, which already owns 91 million acres, a piece much larger than the entire state of Colorado. You'd think that would be enough. But in 1992, a generous Congress appropriated $135 million to buy additional wildlife preserves and land for migratory birds. The same amount of money has been budgeted for 1993.

In an affluent society, with a balanced budget and without crippling debt and interest payments, the people might want to satisfy Uncle Sam's unstoppable appetite for virgin land. But the current spending of hundreds of millions of dollars a year is a great waste for America today, especially with the high prices being paid.

Why not sell off some unwanted federal land and make the money back?

The idea is sound, but as we shall see in the next

section, Uncle Sam follows a unique business pattern. He buys high and sells low.

The solution?

Cool all new land acquisitions until the budget is balanced, and perhaps further into the future. Few fans of the open spaces will ever feel crowded in a government domain that is larger than all of Western Europe.

But if Washington *really* needs more land, I've got a half acre of wetlands in my yard that's perfect for migratory birds. Any bids?

37

LAND, SALES

Sell Low, Buy High

IN OREGON, a clever reader of federal laws learned that for $2.50 an acre, he could buy up vast tracts of federal land by just filing a claim.

The Mining Law of 1872 was originally put into place to explore and develop minerals in the West—to prospect for everything from gold to iron. Anything people found they could keep. Uncle Sam was owed no royalties. All the prospector had to do was put $100 a year into developing the land, after which he could buy it outright at the now ridiculously low price.

Surely, the law has changed dramatically since 1872. Valuable land can't be bought from Uncle Sam for $2.50 an acre. Right? Wrong. Though prices in general have gone up a hundredfold since 1872 ($1500 could buy you a nice house) the law stands just as it was, a legal rip-off of taxpayer money.

In Oregon, someone purchased 780 acres of Oregon coastal dune land from the Bureau of Land Management, which handles this type of sale, for $2.50 an acre, or a total of $1950. Since the dunes contained silica sand used to make glass, the "patent," as the deed is called, fulfilled the mining law's requirements.

When the area was declared a historic seashore—the Oregon Dunes National Recreation Area—the government was highly embarrassed. The parcel it had sold was smack in the center of the new federal zone. The Forest

Service, which handled the land, investigated but found that the sale—if that's what you call it—was strictly according to law.

"We're trying to get the land back," says a Forest Service official in Oregon. "We estimate it's worth about $400,000, but the owners are talking about millions. So far we've offered to exchange some land with them, but we haven't heard. It may end up in court. By law, if we condemn the land, we have to pay fair market value and that's what the courts will decide."

This is only one of many cases of the government's unique theory of "buy high, sell low." As communities reach out farther into undeveloped areas and federal lands become potential resort and tourist sites, more Americans are trying to tap into the archaic bargain.

As of a recent year, 265 applications were on hand for 80,000 acres of public lands. The government would take in a minuscule sum for land that has an appraised value of up to $47 million. Some of the $2.50 parcels near a growing gambling casino town in Nevada are considered worth $200,000 an acre.

In one tragic case for taxpayers, the Department of Interior sold 17,000 acres of public land for $42,500. A few weeks later, the buyer turned around and sold it to an oil company. What did he get? You may have guessed: $37 million.

Solution?

The 1872 law should be changed immediately so that the government sells land only at fair market price.

Land is the government's most valuable asset, and we have plenty of it. But that doesn't mean it has to be given away by an amateur, and quite naive, real-estate agent whose shingle bears the unique slogan: "Sell Low, Buy High."

38

LINE ITEM VETO

The President Strikes Back

OVER THE LAST HALF CENTURY, as Congress has become more adept at thwarting the will of American Presidents, Chief Executives have pined for the "Line Item Veto."

Why? Surely the Constitution, in Article I, Section VII, clearly outlines the President's veto power. He can send any bill to the dustbin with the mere scratch of his pen. In order to make it law, Congress must then "override" the President with a two-thirds vote. That balance between the Executive and Legislative branches, the Founding Fathers thought, would make for a more efficient democracy.

Doesn't it? No, not anymore.

What the founders didn't count on was modern Congresses, of whatever party. They've figured out how to handle recalcitrant Presidents, especially the rare economy-minded type. By bunching up their bills into mammoth monsters, or by adding piquant little amendments that Presidents hate, they have managed to sneak in a lot of what they want without risking a veto.

Only a few years ago, Congress pushed through $600 billion worth of appropriations in one Omnibus Bill. The President's choice was simple: sign it or virtually shut down the government.

Governors have had the same problem with state legislators, but most have solved it handily. In 43 states, the
Governors have the right of Line Item Veto, which means
they can go through any appropriations bill with a sharp
pen and cross out the parts they don't like, then sign on
for the rest. This LIV, as it's called in shorthand, has saved
billions for the states, 49 of which must constitutionally
balance their budgets.

In some states, including Massachusetts and California, the Governor can even keep the sense of the appropriation, but reduce the amount as he sees fit.

Why not do as much for the President?

Witness the recent Intermodal Surface Transportation
Efficiency Act of 1991, which appropriated $153 billion
for roads and mass transit (see HIGHWAYS AND ROADS).
When Congressmen loaded it up with pork, the President was outraged. But afraid to lose the important job-
creating legislation, he knuckled under to clever Representatives.

Why don't our Presidents have the LIV? Actually,
some Constitutional scholars believe they already have
that power, *implicitly*. The theory is that without it, Congress could put all the year's fiscal legislation in one fat
package, then dare the President to veto it.

These constitutional theorists believe all the President
has to do is line item out the extravagant portions of any
bill, then tell Congress that it's been signed into law, if
thinned out by his deletions. The final battle of that war
between the Hill and the Oval Office would, of course,
end up in the Supreme Court.

Others are not sure the President has the implicit
power, but they have offered legislation to give it to the
White House.

Senate sponsors of the LIV have proposed several such

bills. Some grant the President the authority by statute; others require a Constitutional amendment to get around a Supreme Court fight. In 1989, Senate Judiciary Resolutions 14 and 23 asking for a Constitutional amendment were approved by the committee 8–6, supported by both Republicans and Democrats, but have since languished in legislative limbo.

Two Senators are not giving up the fight and are taking the simple legislative route instead of seeking a Constitutional amendment. In January 1991, Senators Dan Coats of Indiana and John McCain of Arizona introduced Senate Bill S 196, the Line Item Veto Act of 1991, which would grant the President the modified right to cut out portions of an appropriations bill, subject to a Congressional second look. By 1992, the bill had 30 sponsors in the Senate.

"What's happened to S 196?" I asked a spokesperson in Coats's office.

"Check with the Senate Documents Office," was the response. "They'll know the exact disposition. They have it all on computer."

I called and asked about the Line Item Veto Act.

"There has been no action on the bill at all," she said after checking the screen. "It was proposed in January 1991, but it's not scheduled for consideration. It's just sitting in the Governmental Affairs Committee."

Instead of waiting (perhaps forever), the two Senators have reworded it and offered it as an amendment to other bills. At their last try, in February 1992, they came closer than ever, losing by a relatively close 44–54 vote in the Senate.

If the bill ever becomes law and Congress grants a President the LIV, even if watered down, what would the Oval Office do with it?

Any President would be on the line to cut expenditures

dramatically. Instead of just carping that Congress is spending too much, he would have to show the nation he really means business.

The solution?

The public should offer to hold any President's coat while he fights it out with Congress, and even the Supreme Court, if necessary. If only to look good near election time, a responsible Republican, Democrat, or Independent President could use the LIV to cut out at least $30 billion a year.

Not bad for the stroke of a pen.

39

LOANS, GOVERNMENT

Big Bank on the Potomac

THE LARGEST BANK in the world, and the sloppiest and most insolvent, is the United States government.

While we're frightened, and properly so, by $400 billion deficits and $4 trillion national debt, no one talks about the $6.3 *trillion* in federal loans and insurance sitting out there, waiting for defaults to ensnare us, as it already has in the S&L crisis.

The credit line is large and growing rapidly, up a half trillion dollars from just a year ago, and up $3.5 trillion in the past ten years, the most hectic period of government-backed debt.

The debtors are virtually everybody—from farmers to students, from foreign corporations to mortgagees, from banks to large corporation pension funds.

The government has been playing tricks on the people by not being frank about this risky loan portfolio. Finally, Washington has admitted that the game of off-budget fiscal hanky-panky is a dangerous one. Says the 1992 budget document: "The dramatic growth of the Government's contingent credit and insurance liabilities is in part due to failure to reflect their true costs in the Federal budget."

What are their true costs? And are you sure you want to know?

Of the $6 trillion involved, the government admits that losses can run as high as $352 *billion* over the next six years, and many believe this is a low-ball estimate. The deposit insurance on banks and S&Ls is figured at up to $161 billion, which is already outdated. Other loans, from students, small business, FHA, VA, farmers, and so on, are calculated at another $191 billion. Judging from experience in government estimates, we can rest assured that the amount will exceed that figure.

The loans and defaults cover the federal waterfront. The largest loss ratio is expected in the direct loan category, where the money comes right out of the federal Treasury. (Or more likely, is borrowed by Washington in order to loan it out.) Of the $162 billion in direct loans, the OMB expects that *almost half*, or $77 billion, could default, all of which will come out of the taxpayer's pocket.

One of the worst offenders is the Export-Import Bank, a strange government operation in which we loan foreign companies money so they can buy our exports. Although it involves only a small part of our whole export picture, the bank costs us billions in cheap interest subsidies and defaults.

"Eximbank sustained large losses over the past decade," says the 1992 budget.

Because we were loaning foreigners money at rates lower than we were paying for it, the bank showed a $2.3 billion loss just in operations. In addition, of the $9 billion out in direct loans, we expect to lose as much as $6 billion—a 66% default rate! Of the guaranteed export loans of $5 billion, we anticipate losing as much as $4 billion. The overall record of the Export-Import Bank is one of near total bankruptcy. So much for our foreign friends.

The answer to the crushing credit drain is fourfold:

(1) Stop *all* direct loans out of Uncle Sam's pocket. Rely only on guaranteed loans that go through banks.

(2) Remember that most of the money loaned out has been borrowed *by* Washington in the first place. Stop all subsidy loans. Raise the interest rate to slightly more than we're paying for the money.

(3) Close down the Export-Import Bank. Financing foreign importers who don't pay their bills is not bright.

(4) Cut out completely, or drastically reduce, loans in several of the programs. We've already seen see some of the worst deadbeats at work, and more will follow. All demonstrate that Uncle Sam is a foolish lender who apparently doesn't understand that while the bureaucrats may make the loans, it's the taxpayers who end up holding the empty black bag.

40

MARKETING, BIG BUSINESS

Ads on the House

THE SLICK FOUR-COLOR ADVERTISEMENT in a popular Japanese magazine showed an urban cowboy dressed in Wrangler jeans.

Why the expensive advertisement? For two reasons. First, blue jeans have become the rage of sophisticated Japanese men. And second, why not? The Wrangler ad was paid for by the American taxpayer.

Couldn't Wrangler afford to handle the advertisement themselves? Surely. The company grosses $550 million a year, but that's a comparatively small operation. The ad was actually run by their licensee, Wrangler of Japan, a Japanese-owned firm, one of whose partners is the giant conglomerate Mitsubishi. Despite that, the American government gave Wrangler of Japan a gift of $1.1 million to advertise their blue jeans.

Again why? And to a foreign company?

It all began in 1990, when Congress authorized the Department of Agriculture to spend $1 *billion* of our money, $200 million a year for five years, to subsidize advertising of American agricultural products overseas, even if the money went to foreign firms. As part of this government "Market Promotion Program," the Wrangler ad was used to promote the sale of American cotton.

Last year, 630 brands, scores of them foreign, took the Treasury up on its generous offer. Were they struggling firms who got the government dole?

No way. The largest amounts went to mammoth corporations with the least need, all of whom gladly accepted the taxpayer's handout. Please read this roster, a Who's Who of food products, and the amounts of their advertising tabs picked up by Uncle Sam:

Gallo Wines ($5.1 million); Sunkist citrus products ($9.9 million); Blue Diamond Almonds ($6.2 million); McDonald's ($465,000); Pillsbury, actually a British-owned company ($2.9 million); Tyson chickens ($1.1 million); Ralston-Purina ($200,000); Dole ($2,450,000); Ocean Spray ($1 million); Welch's ($1,214,000); Hunt-Wesson ($235,750); Kraft ($100,000); Campbell Soups ($450,000). Even Paul Newman's "Newman's Own" received a federal gift of $100,000.

The Department of Agriculture, which often serves as the arm of the powerful farm lobby, claims that American firms made back more than the expenditure. Even if true, which can hardly be measured, that's *our* tax money going out to the big corporations, and *their* money coming in. This is not a loan, but a federal grant.

And what about the cost of this extraordinary corporate welfare at a time of a $400 billion deficit?

As D of A economists and dollar-blind Congressmen should know, if we borrow that $1 billion today for this giveaway—as we are doing—by the time the 30-year government bonds, at 8% interest, mature in 2022, it will have cost the taxpayers almost *$4 billion*.

Anyone for too-tight Wranglers?

41

MEDICAID

Washington Orders, States Pay

"OUR MEDICAID COSTS for 1992 are 20% higher than they were last year, and they're going to go up another 20% in 1993," says a Medicaid official in Connecticut. "The federal government mandates what kind of care we have to provide, and which people we have to cover, but we have to put up half the money. We can't afford it."

That Medicaid cost has reached almost $2 billion in Connecticut, or $1200 in state taxes for the average family of four, few of whom get any of the health care. The program benefits only 8% of the state's residents, but is the fastest growing item in this, and every state's, budget. Nationwide, the bill is now $117 billion, and the tunnel shows no evidence of light at the end.

How did it get this way?

The typical Medicaid patient is poor, often a recipient of Aid to Families with Dependent Children (AFDC), and a single mother as head of the household. Depending on the state, the program also includes some unemployed people with few assets who have lost their health insurance with their jobs. But most states have strict eligibility rules for poor working people, or those who have lost their jobs.

"The family applying for Medicaid can have a home—

although we put a lien on it after a few months—and a car," explains a Connecticut Medicaid official. "But their car can't be worth more than $1500 in the Blue Book. If it's more than that, they have to sell their own car and buy a cheap used one."

Medicaid is the wild card in the crazy game of government medical care that includes Medicaid, Medicare, Veterans Hospitals and clinics, the National Institutes of Health, health research grants, the Public Health Service, and Indian Health Care. Altogether it adds up to about $300 billion a year, almost 40% of our total health bill. Yet it bypasses the great bulk of the American people.

In the case of Medicaid, Washington pulls the strings and the states jump through fiscal hoops.

"Medicaid recently mandated that we raise the reimbursement rates for doctors in OB-GYN to 90% of the prevailing fees so that poor pregnant mothers on AFDC could get better care, including prenatal attention," says a Connecticut spokesman. "That cost us a lot of money."

Medicaid and Medicare, both passed in 1965, are the two largest items in the federal health budget, and the fastest growing. In 1992, they accounted for a quarter *trillion* dollars, and rose at the rate of 20% a year, which is the Chapter 11 equivalent of health care. In the case of Medicaid, the rolls continue to grow at that rate because of new clients and the recession.

Despite the enormous bill, most Medicaid fees are set so low that many doctors refuse to treat the patients, which is the reason for the reimbursement hike for poor pregnant mothers. Hospitals and emergency rooms cannot generally refuse Medicaid patients, which is another reason for the higher costs. For many Medicaid patients, the hospital is their family doctor.

But nursing homes, generally covered by states under Medicaid for the indigent aged, present a different problem. There the reimbursement is too *high*. In Connecticut, for example, there are 18,000 older people in private profit-making nursing homes, paid in full by Medicaid. The cost for each patient is $41,000 a year plus doctors' bills. In all, with administration, it approaches $50,000 a patient. As the population ages, the number housed in these profit-making institutions will rise, along with the astronomical bill.

"We are trying home care with some of the aged, when possible, which costs only $11,000, but that's not usually feasible," says a Connecticut spokesman.

Some states are tackling the Medicaid problem medically, if in no other way. Arizona, which initially had not been in the Medicaid program, has now installed AHCCS, pronounced "Access," which stands for Arizona Health Care Cost System.

"It's a managed care system which includes all Medicaid patients," says an Arizona spokesman. "The clients choose from one of several HMO plans, where they get total care, including a primary doctor and a group of specialists."

Is it too expensive? I asked.

"Actually, a study done by an outside organization indicates that it's cheaper, by 5%, than the regular fee-for-service Medicaid systems in other states," says the AHCCS spokesman. "Our problem is that some taxpaying citizens are annoyed because the poor—including illegal aliens—are getting better care than they are, and they're paying for the whole program."

In some states, the HMOs, like U.S. Healthcare, are considered a good medical and administrative solution, but they are often too expensive. "We had a few HMOs taking care of our Medicaid patients, but they dropped us because they weren't making any money," says a Connecticut official.

The complexity of the Medicaid dilemma is a microcosm of the larger medical and health insurance problem in America. At its base are the excessive costs of doctor and hospital care, and the lack of planning, at all levels.

What's the solution?

Obviously, it requires the end of piecemeal handling of the question. Medicaid cannot be fixed unless the whole picture—which takes one out of every seven dollars in America—is fixed.

Is there a model for an overall health insurance scheme?

Possibly. Not Britain, of course. Perhaps Canada, if one prefers a single insurer—the government. But there are two others as well: Germany, which has made enormous strides in social service, and France, both of which are providing health care for all without breaking the bank. We'll soon take a peek at these two possibilities.

There's a lot of disagreement about future models for a national health-care system in America. But almost everyone agrees on one point. Uncontained, uncontrolled, poorly designed Medicaid is not one of them.

42

MEDICARE

A Runaway Operation

THE NEW SENIOR CITIZEN received a list of the internists in Westchester County, New York, who would supposedly accept the Medicare assignment, meaning they would take the government allowance as full payment.

A quick check of the list produced these incredible results: Almost all the physicians contacted were either (1) dead, (2) retired, or (3) no longer accepting Medicare assignments. One of the few exceptions was the New York Medical College, whose faculty was already receiving regular salaries.

This snafu is only one symptom of a system that is among the most needed of government services, yet among the most wasteful.

During the past five years, Medicare costs have risen an annual average of 13%, three times the rate of inflation, with no prospect of a leveling off. The program, which now serves 35 million aged, costs $131 billion a year and is headed for $226 billion in 1997. The crippling rise is caused by several factors, especially fiscally careless hospitals and, to put it charitably, money-conscious doctors.

Surely, we say, part of it has to be due to the graying of America. No?

Not really. In the 1991–93 period, as Medicare rolls increased only 4%, costs rose 23%.

What's the government doing to stop this hemorrhaging? Very little.

"Over the last six to seven years, they've been trying different payment mechanisms to cut costs," says a government specialist in Medicare, "but so far they haven't reduced physician fees."

The result, he says, is that doctors' compensation goes up some 15% per year, rising from $2 billion in 1975 to $40 billion today. Medicare used to pay doctors the "prevailing" fees in their area. Now they have changed to a "relative value system," which they say makes it more equitable. That is, a family doctor in rural Kansas will get more beginning in 1992 and the Park Avenue specialist less.

But will it benefit the patient or the federal budget? No way.

"The system was designed to be revenue neutral," says a Medicare official in Washington. Translation? Doctors will still extract their usual pound from our senior citizens.

But what the government has done is to keep raising the cost to both taxpayers and the aged. A few years ago, everyone got a Medicare payroll tax increase. It used to be 1.45% of earnings up to about $55,000, but it now has an income ceiling of $130,000, a figure that goes up each year with the GNP.

Similarly, the premiums paid by seniors on Part B of Medicare, which is strictly for doctor reimbursement, also keep rising.

Washington seems more afraid of the special interests—the doctors, the AMA and the hospitals—than they are of voters or the aged, who are still not fully clued in to the medical scam.

No matter what dollar amount is put on their fee schedule, physicians can make all the money they want off Washington and the aged simply by performing more procedures on each patient. They are not paid per person, as in an HMO, but for each treatment and part of treatment—costs that continue to escalate.

Hospitals are another problem. Medicare doesn't pay them for exact services rendered, as we would think. They actually help support the hospitals, almost as if they were federal institutions, a wasteful practice that costs us additional billions each year.

"The Health Care Financing Administration—Medicare and Medicaid—pay about 40% of the entire cost of running a typical hospital," explains a government spokesman. "They don't pay for the time patients spend there, but give the hospital a flat sum for a gall bladder or pneumonia or heart by-pass. But Medicare also pays for capital improvements, high-tech equipment, salaries of interns and residents, even medical education. All that comes out of the Medicare budget."

Using Medicare funds for what used to be handled by private charity is one reason for rising costs. It's also responsible for the growth of unneeded hospitals. In fact, the U.S. has the highest hospital-bed vacancy rate in the developed world. On any given day, according to the American Hospital Association, 35% of our hospital beds are empty, which also adds to the swollen Medicare bill.

There are many wasteful practices pushing up Medicare costs. Teaching hospitals, for example, receive an extra $2.5 billion from Medicare each year, payments that are too high. Another giant waste comes from diagnostic labs, which often take advantage of the careless government. "Payments for their test services remain too high," says a report. "Discounts are offered to physicians and other providers, but not to Medicare." A review of five labs showed a profit margin of 32% on Medicare patients as against the usual 15%.

America rightly boasts of such high-tech equipment as CAT scans and MRI imagers, but boosters fail to point out that much of the tab is picked up by near-bankrupt Medicare. Once the device is declared eligible for Medicare reimbursement, hospital officials rush out and buy it, even if there's one just like it a half mile away. In 1985, fewer than 100 MRI units were available in America. Today there are 3000, and Medicare pays $458 each time a scan is taken, well above the actual cost. Together with CAT scans, that runs Medicare hundreds of millions of dollars a year.

Another bleeding sore in the Medicare (and Medicaid) body is simple fraud. Too many hospitals and doctors cheat, and money stolen from the system is estimated at $20 to $40 billion a year.

"Our adversaries in this arena are often well-educated health-care professionals who have surrendered to greed and prey on those least able to protect themselves," says Judge William Sessions, director of the FBI, which is expanding its unit dealing with Medicare fraud.

"Some doctors not only invent procedures they've never done, but some even invent patients and patient visits," says a criminal investigator in HCFA. "Another big fraud is perpetrated by hospitals. They falsely shift costs from the private to the public operations of their hospital and put in large fake claims to Medicare."

Last year, HCFA alone conducted 1168 successful actions against shifty providers. There were 163 criminal convictions, including 26 doctors.

What's the answer to the spiraling costs?

It's really quite simple. We need a new plan.

We can use the Canadian system of a single insurer—the government. Or we can go to the multi-insurance system of Germany and France. Germany is a model for controlling doctor costs while France is noted for checking rising hospital charges.

Health care in both countries costs only 9% of the GNP as against 14% here (headed for 16%), and virtually everyone is insured. As in America, patients have a free choice of doctors and hospitals.

In Germany, health insurance is compulsory. Coverage is provided on the job by all employers. The unemployed and self-employed are covered by the same insurers—90% of whom are nonprofit versus only 40% here. Health insurers cannot charge different rates or offer less, or select out a healthier or younger population. The risk is spread over large groups of people, not just a single workplace or an individual.

The real genius of their plan is the strict control of *doctor* costs. Fees for specific procedures are set by region. The doctors cannot charge more, or accept extra money. There is very little co-insurance, and a patient's cash outlay is minimal.

But can't doctors get around that by increasing the number of procedures on each patient, thus making more money? And by doing it nationally—as American doctors do—outfox the entire health plan?

No. Bonn has outfoxed the cagey doctors. The government puts a *"cap"* on payouts to doctors for the year. As the volume of bills goes up, the computers churn back. The payments go down, so that at the end of the year, the cap is what they've paid out.

The French have done something similar to hold down hospital costs.

Like the Germans, they regulate hospital construction and the buying of high-tech equipment. But they have added another fillip that truly holds the line.

Their private hospitals (*cliniques*) get a set per diem rate per patient regardless of what treatment is done. It's the same for all insurers and is negotiated each year. For public hospitals (in America that would include voluntary and community hospitals) the government and the "sickness funds" negotiate the *entire budget* of the hospital.

That keeps the bills from skyrocketing as they do in America, where Medicare and Medicaid funds only feed the hospital's ambition for expansion and gives them a chance to sneakily "cost shift" expenses away from private patients onto the federal government.

Will this work with American doctors and hospitals?

Not if you ask them. Hospitals have to start submitting to regional planning and regulation. Otherwise we're headed for bankruptcy. The French system of getting heavily involved in setting the hospital budget is the only solution.

How about the American doctors?

Medicare is a good place to start teaching them that medical practice is a public trust. Put in the German plan of set fees and capped total payout and watch the rising physician costs come to a screeching halt.

Meanwhile:

(1) Medicare should scale back its support of hospitals by cutting out payment for capital expenditures. It only encourages unneeded hospital expansion.

(2) The government cannot afford to pick up the tab for medical education, which should be removed as a Medicare reimbursement.

(3) High-tech equipment such as MRI machines should not be supported by Medicare without prior planning, the only way to eliminate expensive duplication.

(4) Medicare should use its power as a giant customer to drastically reduce its payments to diagnostic laboratories.

(5) Medicare must take the lead in consolidating hospitals and eliminating the excess number of unused beds.

(6) Even more attention should be placed on cutting down doctor and hospital fraud.

(7) Medicare (and Medicaid) must cut out the hospital racket of shifting costs from private usage to Uncle Sam's checkbook.

(8) Last, but not least, Medicare has to set a tight fee schedule for doctors and not permit them to charge a dollar more or take *any* money from senior citizens.

With that threat and the possibility of a *cap* over their heads, what can our inordinately wealthy doctors do?

Actually, they can easily outwit us. All they need do is pile their family into the car and drive to Toronto, Canada, where they can set up a new practice—and earn even less.

Or, in absolute desperation, they can emigrate to Britain, where they'll quickly learn just how little doctors can be paid.

Anyone for a used Lexus?

43

MILITARY PENSIONS

Want to Retire Real Young?

SERGEANT JOHN Q. SOLDIER IS thirty-eight years old and is *finishing* his career in the United States Army, after having put in twenty years.

What is his reward? Is he being discarded by the government he served so honorably, and left to drift on his own resources?

You bet he's not. Sergeant Soldier, who is retiring as an E-9, the top enlisted specialist grade, can look forward to one of the earliest and best pensions in the nation, government or private. He will have a lifetime of relative security, with his former employers guiding him all the way. Of course, the price to his civilian counterpart, the over-stretched Mr. Taxpayer, is quite steep.

As a former E-9, Mr. Soldier receives Social Security when the time comes, and he makes his payroll deduction like everyone else. But unlike anyone else, he contributes absolutely *nothing* to his military retirement plan. That's picked up strictly by you and me.

His pay scale, including allotments, will be $42,047 per annum his last year in the service, but his pension is based upon his base pay of $31,512. Twenty-year men like him, retiring long before they even reach the prime of life, will get 40% of that amount—or $12,605 a year plus an annual cost of living increase.

Should Sergeant Soldier decide to stay in until he's forty-eight, with 30 years' service, his retirement pay jumps rapidly up to $24,000 a year, plus COLAS (cost-of-living adjustments). At his final retirement at age sixty-five, the pension will be about $50,000 a year, which is added to his Social Security payments.

But at forty-eight, he's still young enough to reenter the job market. Along with his salary, he'll be vesting a second pension, a procedure known as "double dipping." He might even get a government job, which will "restrict" him to $104,000 in combined salary and pension. But if he works for an outside firm, even a defense contractor, there's no cap.

What does all this cost the taxpayer? Mr. Soldier's pension from age forty-eight to his death twenty-nine years later will run $750,000 in current dollars and about $1.5 million in future dollars. Not bad for a pension to which he contributed nothing.

Officers, of course, receive considerably more. A chicken colonel, retiring at age fifty-one, after West Point and 30 years of service, is making $80,743 a year, with a base pay of $65,000. His retirement pay is $49,000, which will cost Uncle Sam a total of some $1.4 million in current dollars.

In all, there are 1.5 million retired military personnel, who continue in the relative security of a service life, just as if they were still on active duty.

After they leave, they receive a retiree ID card. It's no golden parachute, but it's strong enough to keep them afloat—a kind of paternalistic socialism in a capitalist world. The retiree and his or her family have access to all military bases and the use of discount military commissaries, post exchanges, golf courses, tennis courts, and swimming pools, as well as officers' and non-com clubs.

The retirees continue to get free medical treatment on base for themselves and dependents, and they and their dependents are insured, free of charge, for medical care off the base.

The pensions needn't end with death. For a small fee, the monthly pension will go to their beneficiaries until they also reach retirement age.

If he's so inclined, ex-Sergeant Soldier can go back to college. The GI Bill, into which he has paid a total of $1200 (a requirement put in by Jerry Ford) will grant him $300 a month for schooling for 36 months. In the case of 125,000 GIs who made a good bargain with the recruiter, they have what is called a "kicker." These GIs get $700 a month for 36 months, a $25,000 education package.

Just like the federal civilian employee, the retired military person gets another present from Uncle Sam when he reaches sixty-two. Any penalty he suffered for leaving before 30 years of service is restored. So the retiree who got only a 40% pension has now automatically been elevated to 50%, an extra few thousand dollars a year.

Military pensions now cost taxpayers $22 billion a year, which is not Welsh rarebit. But the real pain for the Treasury is up ahead. The plan is not really funded, leaving the enormous liability—already $622 billion and rising—for the future taxpayer. There is only $80 billion in the kitty, and the liability rises faster than the cash, soon approaching a *trillion* dollars.

It takes a Scrooge not to wish our ex-military personnel well. But Christmas is virtually every day for the retired soldier and sailor, and maybe—just maybe—we the taxpayers have turned into poor Bob Cratchit.

What to do?

(1) Discontinue free medical care and health insurance for service retirees and their dependents. They will re-

ceive it at their new jobs, or can *buy* it from the military retiree plan.

(2) Have all service people contribute to their pension plans through payroll deductions. Should they stay 20 years or more, they'll still come out way ahead.

(3) If they leave before 20 years, their retirement deductions, plus accrued interest, should be returned to them like a savings plan.

(4) The 75% pension for 30 years of military service is excessive and should be cut down to 50%, especially since they're also covered for Social Security.

(5) Some officer pensions are too high.

(6) The COLAS on pensions, year after year, are too expensive for any Treasury, particularly when the retiree did not contribute to the plan.

How much will this all save? Probably as much as $9 billion a year—and growing.

We should be proud of our military personnel, active and retired. But as patriots, they shouldn't want to contribute to the fiscal agony of America.

And besides, we're jealous of anyone who can retire before forty.

44

MILK

Sucking at the Federal Teat

In 1983, even the bureaucrats in Washington became frightened.

Almost a half century before, they had instituted a milk subsidy program to keep dairy farmers down on the farm and keep milk production and milk prices up. The scheme was simple: the government would buy any milk the dairy farmers couldn't sell, at prices higher than the market. Since milk is perishable, the farmers had to convert it into cheese, butter, and dry milk. The government both stored it and gave it away.

But in '83, the program was awash in milk. Encouraged by high subsidies, which have risen dramatically in the last 20 years, farmers produced far beyond the nation's needs. Then they put in the bill—$2.6 billion ($5 billion in today's dollars) and collected from Washington.

What to do?

In 1985, Congress passed the Dairy Termination Program, which bears an unfortunate similarity to Schwarzenegger's character. For every cow they killed or sold for export, farmers would receive approximately $2000 from the government, plus whatever they got paid for the meat. They also had to promise to go on a farm furlough—to leave the business for five years. For this the average farmer got a check for $128,000, and the big producers much more.

The combined activity—decimation and termination—the government theorized, would slow milk production considerably.

What happened? The first result was that the price of beef dropped drastically and cattle farmers, who were not subsidized, lost $25 million in a flash. The second result was that the government had to pay out $1.8 billion more in 1986–87, above the subsidies, for the "termination" program.

And what happened to milk production from 1985 on? Perhaps not so surprisingly, it *increased*, from 140 billion pounds in 1985 to 146 billion in 1988. In addition, a sizable number of the farmers who were bought out—with their equipment intact—say they intend to return to dairy farming now that the five years are up.

As government auditors comment: "The estimates of annual reductions declined each year after 1987, indicating that the program would not have a lasting effect on milk production."

That all followed a prior federal boondoggle that tried to distort normal economics. This one was called the Milk Diversion Program, a double subsidy program. In 1984 and '85, Washington paid farmers not only for their surplus, but extra money to reduce their output.

The auditors again revealed the government folly. "We stated that . . . milk sales could rebound to pre-program levels after the program's expiration. This in fact happened."

One of the funniest—or most tragic—elements of the plan is that the government sets the minimum price for most milk, and penalizes farmers of the Upper Midwest—the center of the dairy business—because they are where they are. Using the "Eau Claire" [Wisconsin] law, dairy farmers get larger subsidies the farther they are from that productive town. The result is that the once-great center of the dairy business is weakening, and cheaper areas like the Southwest are growing.

What is the bottom line on the half-century-old program?

It was a New Deal operation, which in its time was needed and successful. It kept millions of dairy farmers from going broke and increased milk production.

But today? It's asinine. It has cost the government $20 billion in subsidies and raised milk prices to consumers $40 billion. The natural laws of economics have ruled the business anyway, and the 5 million dairy farms have virtually disappeared despite subsidies, or even because of the way they favored big producers. In their place there are only 220,000 dairy farms, a number that drops each year as herds get bigger and each cow gives more milk, courtesy of modern machinery and breeding.

The government knows nothing about dairy farming and shouldn't be in the business. If they get out of it, farmers will produce just enough milk to sell at the right price, and the taxpayers will save a billion dollars a year.

Are we ready for "Termination II?"

45

NATIONAL ARCHIVES

The Paper Chase

THE LIVING HISTORY of our nation is intriguing, and as one who has taught history, I find it particularly exciting. But the way the federal government has thrown itself into the subject is, in the final analysis, silly and enormously wasteful.

In 1934, Washington set up the National Archives to maintain historical records of the federal government, something that had been virtually overlooked for the first 150 years of the Republic.

The oversight has been corrected, and like most government projects, has senselessly exploded in the process. Today, the Archives have become the collector of thousands of tons of paper, squirreling it away in depositories and cataloguing it at great cost to the taxpayer. And in the process, they are giving once-modest history an expensive name.

"We have fourteen depositories for our records around the country," explains a National Archives spokesperson. "Our appraisers go into each of the federal agencies to determine what should be kept. Overall, I'd say we save about 1% of all the paperwork."

One percent? In the expanding paper chase of modern Washington, that small percentage comes to 1.8 *million* cubic feet each year, equal to an entire football field (360 × 160 feet) covered with paper, then piled 37 feet high!

How much government paper is being held in all fourteen centers around the country?

"Since 1970," proudly states the Archives' annual report, "records holdings have increased from 10.5 million to 16.9 million cubic feet, an increase of 60.9%."

Using the football field analogy, that makes a pile covering the entire turf, going up 352 feet into the air.

Does this program of paper-saving cost us as much as $10 million a year?

Guess again. The 1992 budget for the National Archives is $165 million, quite an appropriation for document housing, historical or otherwise. (In addition, reveals the Office of Personnel and Management, the government has 663 historians on the payroll, at a cost of some $50 million.)

Two hundred million dollars a year for government paper and history—evidentiary, legal, and fiscal?

Again, that's nothing.

"We're now headquartered on Pennsylvania Avenue, in a block-square building," says the spokesperson, "but we need more room so we're constructing a new building—Archives II—on the University of Maryland campus in College Park."

Another $10–20 million to make sure that posterity knows the intimate details of the peanut subsidy program of 1978?

Guess again, amateur historians. That new building, which will be completed in 1994, will cost the taxpayers *$300 million.*

The National Archives are also the repository of "classified" documents going back 20, 30 years, and more. The agencies and the Archives regularly declassify them as years go on, but the Archives are still exploding with tons of "secret" documents, few of which have any meaning today.

Solution?

Sharpen the eyes of the appraisers and cut the yearly intake of paper down by 90%. Then have them reinspect the contents of the main center and the fourteen depositories, keeping only one-tenth of the inventory, at the very most. Declassify 95% of the material as meaningless in today's world. Then close down three-quarters of the paper-crammed warehouses.

Cut the staff from its extravagant 2086 to a modest 500, and reduce the budget of the National Archives to $25 million over a period of years, a savings of $140 million per annum. Move the whole operation to College Park and rent out their offices on high-rent Pennsylvania Avenue.

Nothing better expresses the hubris of a Congress, Presidency, and federal bureaucracy unable to understand the true needs of the nation than the operation of this mad paper chase.

What about the most monumental bonfire in history?

46

NEWSLETTERS

On the House

THE NEXT TIME you open your mailbox and take out a fancy newsletter from your Congressman, his smiling visage looking up at you, think about the fact that *everyone* in the United States is getting a similar one from their Representative.

Members of the House are allowed to send this clever public-relations device to constituents as often as they can manage, supposedly to keep voters informed. The "news" is problematic, but the astronomical cost to taxpayers for this self-serving brochure is real.

Let's do a little arithmetic. The typical member of Congress represents 585,000 people, and has about 250,000 households on his precious mailing list. To print and address the newsletter costs about 8 cents apiece, or $60,000 for three a year, the usual amount. For the House as a whole, that's a bill for $26 million.

What about the postage? Congressmen have a yearly mail allowance that averages $200,000. About 60% of this goes to mail his constituent missives, or $120,000.

Now for a little multiplication. Since there are 435 of these people in the House of Representatives, the mailing cost for the newsletters is $52 million. Add that to the printing and we get a total of $78 million per year, in the

House alone. That's a lot of money for what is actually a reelection gimmick.

But isn't Congressional mail free? When we see the frank without a stamp on mailings from Congress, we assume that somehow there is no cost.

"No," explains a House Finance Office spokesman. "The mail is all bundled and the actual postage tallied. Then we send a check to the Post Office to pay for it just like anyone else."

What can be done to curb this excess?

The simplest remedy is for the House to first pass legislation cutting its newsletter mailings to *one* per year. Then, with a little arm twisting by voters, perhaps Congress could be convinced to *totally eliminate* them, which would mean we could pocket the whole $78 million.

Representatives might be somewhat less in touch with their constituents, but I doubt that many of us will grieve. It might even have a salutary side effect by breaking the grip incumbents have had on the House.

In any case, taxpayers will be thankful to bank $78 million in place of the little missives they never asked for in the first place.

47

NONPROFIT ORGANIZATIONS

Charity for All, Please

AMERICANS ARE very charitable. We voluntarily contribute over $100 billion a year to various not-for-profit organizations.

Few people know that the federal government also distributes $4 billion of our tax money to these same private groups in the form of grants. But even fewer are aware that there is another hidden subsidy for nonprofit organizations, *in addition* to the $15 billion in taxes they do not pay.

It's a mail subsidy. If you feel overwhelmed by charity solicitations that come in your postbox, blame it on that.

The Post Office gives them, and political organizations, a discount for bulk mail of some 25–30%. That comes in the form of a "revenue forgone appropriation," which Congress pays the Post Office to make up for the cheaper mail. In 1991, that check was for a substantial *$370 million*.

What should be done?

(1) We should drop political groups entirely from the subsidized mail program.

(2) The price break should be cut in half for regular charities, which are already tax free.

(3) The $4 billion in federal grants should be examined

more carefully. Donations for private charities should be a voluntary action by individuals and businesses, not one ordered by Congress with our tax funds.

The savings? At least several hundred million dollars a year.

The charity, unfortunately, is desperately needed at home.

48

OVERHEAD

The Abnormal Cost of
Doing Business

"WE'VE NEVER DONE a study of federal overhead. We don't know how much it is."

This surprising statement comes from a spokesman in the President's Office of Management and Budget (OMB), the agency in charge of planning how much the federal government spends. Not only doesn't Washington know how much is being spent on overhead—rent, telephone, supplies, travel, copying, et cetera—but they apparently don't want to know. Or let the public in on the secret.

"When we went to OMB to try to pin down the size of the overhead, they gave us very short shrift," says an aide to Congressman Lamar Smith of Texas, a cost-conscious Representative who seeks to take over the mantle of the retired Senator William Proxmire of Wisconsin, creator of the Golden Fleece Award. "We almost had to force our way into the OMB library to get the information we needed. They wanted no part of our attempt to discover what's obvious in any other business. They were absolutely uncooperative."

In the corporate world, controllers know—to the penny—how large their overhead costs are. Without that knowledge, it would be impossible to price a product or know what cuts to make to turn a profit.

But the federal government, which charges (taxes) whatever it can get away with, has no desire to let the public know its true costs. Examination of the 1992 budget dramatizes the problem. Overhead is not broken out in any recognizable form. In fact, the largest overhead category in the thousands of budget entries is a mysterious "Other Services," which hides a multitude of government sins and tells the taxpayer nothing.

"That's exactly the intention of the OMB," says Congressman Smith's aide. "But we went through all the OMB records and after weeks came up with the answers."

How much does the government actually spend on overhead?

Congressman Smith's estimate is staggering. The United States government spends *$270 billion a year* on overhead, more than the entire annual budget of France. The secretive "Other Services" item totaled $170 billion itself.

His suggestion is to cut that figure by 10% immediately, which would save $27 billion a year. But other observers (including this writer) believe that 25% would be an easily attainable goal. That would mean an almost immediate $68 billion annual reduction in the federal deficit. Later on, as government manpower is appreciably reduced, the overhead reduction could be even more substantial.

"U.S. government spending is totally out of control," says Congressman Smith's aide. "It needs radical restructuring. Some people say that's impossible, but I say that the notion that our government can't be changed—for the better—is absolutely intolerable to a free people."

49

PACS

Including the Secret Ones

PAC IS AN ACRONYM that stands for "Political Action Committee," a money-raising vehicle for elections—state office, Congress, and the Presidency. But its true meaning is "Special Interest."

By some stretch of political imagination, the government thought it was more democratic to raise money for political campaigns under an umbrella rather than directly. The result has been chaos and subterfuge, instead of increased democracy.

There are 4700 PACs, and they raised $372 million and spent $357 million last year. They are organized over the entire special-interest spectrum: corporations; labor unions; health, membership, and trade associations; cooperatives; private corporations without stock; even nonconnected PACs.

They can usually give candidates up to $5000, which makes them popular with politicians. Surely, they are the lifeblood of Washington lobbyists.

What are the largest well-known PACs? The leaders are the Teamsters' Union, $10.5 million; the AMA, $5.7 million; Realtors, $5.3 million; and AT&T, $3.0 million.

These are big, brash, and in the open. But there are sneaky ones as well, which, quite legally, hide their true identity. These are the secret PACs run mainly by prominent people who prefer to remain anonymous. Behind that screen, they can raise small fortunes and donate $5000 to as many candidates as they want.

Most of the "secret" PACs carry exotic, high-sounding patriotic names such as "Participation 2000" or "Campaign Democracy," and even the "I Love America Committee." The sponsors are mainly Congressmen, Senators, Presidents, former Presidents, and Presidential candidates, but their names appear nowhere. Instead, the PACs are registered in the names of friends and relatives.

But are they really kept secret?

By a strange twist of bureaucratic logic, one branch of the government snitches on the other. The Federal Election Commission publishes a list of these secret PACs sponsors, along with the disclaimer: "This is an *UNOFFICIAL* list to be used only as a research tool to locate certain political committees, organizations, or foundations reportedly associated with 'recognized' individuals. . . . The information is compiled by the FEC Press Office from media reports and not official agency records."

From the media to the government, then back to the press. All, mind you, quite "unofficial."

On the list are the names of scores of Congressmen and Senators—in fact, practically every well-known member of both the House and Senate, and the past three Presidents.

The federal election laws, which were last revised in 1974, combine regulation of public, individual, and PAC monies. Unfortunately, they have become a crazy quilt of rules that few of the public understand, and often make no logical sense.

For example, there is a supposed $1000 limit for individual contributions to a political campaign. The reality, however, is that individuals can give *$20,000 each year* to national party committees. The money is then used, softly and cleverly, to help the candidate in various ways, including selected registration and "Get Out the Vote" campaigns. In addition, individuals can donate $5000 a year to PACs, which can then pass it on to the candidate.

PACs may give $5000 to candidates *if* the PAC contributes to five or more candidates (of the same party if they want), but they can also donate money—$15,000 a year—to national party committees. They can even give $5000 to other PACs, and many do. Single candidate PACs may only give candidates $1000, but they can also donate $20,000 to a national party and $5000 to other PACs.

If anyone understands it all.

One clever PAC wrinkle is the quite legal and often-used practice of one politician contributing to another.

What's the purpose?

Power in the legislature or Presidency. If a "Leader," as in Speaker, Minority, or Majority Leader, or Whip, collects bundles of money under his PAC umbrella, he can support the campaigns of fellow Senators and Representatives, thus gaining their allegiance. He may even contribute to such local politicians as the Governor and state legislators, keeping the home territory happy in case a primary against him should arise.

What can be done to straighten out this financial-political mess?

We should *eliminate* all PACs, at the national, state, and local levels. Contributions to candidates and political parties should be limited by law to $250 and $500 respectively, which must come *only* from individuals. (Jerry

Brown made an impetuous but solid contribution to American politics with his "800" number and $100 limit.)

The elimination of PACs from the election scene will cut lobbying power in half with a single stroke. Lobbyists may cajole and even threaten, but without the carrot of PAC money, their control of much of what happens in Washington will disappear.

What will be the result? The present overbearing, stifling power of $350 million in special-interest money will be no more, and those funds can be put back into the normal economy. The federal government will also save millions in Federal Election Commission administration of PAC funds.

Most important, much of the election process will return to the people, where it belongs.

Long live democracy.

50

PENSIONS, BUSINESS

Big Perks for Mighty Corps

WHEN PAN AMERICAN AIRWAYS went belly-up in 1991, the public was dismayed. But at least, they consoled themselves, it wouldn't cost the taxpayers money.

Don't be so sure. It turned out that Pan American's employee pension fund had $900 million less in its coffers than was needed to pay for retirements, and Uncle Sam had to step in.

The federal Pension Benefit Guaranty Corporation insures 40 million employees against loss in 85,000 different pension plans, and increasingly, the government has had to make good. Since the plan went into effect in 1974, the pensions of 1650 bankrupt and weak companies—with not enough money put away—have been taken over by Washington, which now regularly pays out to 372,000 people.

The government collects insurance premiums, so for many years the PBGC felt secure. Unlike the S&Ls, they thought, there would always be enough money to cover their losses.

But no longer.

"We must stem the increase in pension under-funding before we have a crisis," says the director of the PBGC.

The government stands to be stuck with up to $40 billion in what are called "under-funded" pension plans. The government insurance pool already shows a deficit of $2.5 billion.

During 1991, the government took $1 billion in losses, mainly from the bankruptcies of Eastern and Pan Am airlines, and there are still hundreds of shaky companies that could produce an S&L-like bleeding.

Who's the villain? There are two: (1) large corporations who don't put a dollar in the bank for each dollar they promise their workers in pensions; and (2) the federal government, which lets them get away with it.

This "under-funding" is not just practiced by fly-by-nights. According to the PBGC, many major firms are making only minimum contributions to their employee plans and are also "using their pension plans as cheap compensation and a source of low cost 'loans.'" Adds the PBGC director: "In too many cases, we wind up absorbing those loans and writing them off."

Whose pension plans have already been thrown onto the federal insurance plate?

"It includes well-known companies who have gone out of business without enough pension money to take care of their retired people," says a government spokesman. "For example: Wheeling-Pittsburgh Steel, Allis-Chalmers, Braniff Airlines. There are also several troubled companies in Chapter 11 right now who are under-funded—like TWA, which is almost a billion dollars short. If they go under, we'll have to pick up the payments on their pension plan."

Are the under-funded American firms all weak and trembling and in need of federal support?

Hardly. The PBGC has just published a list of the "TOP

50" under-funded firms. Surprisingly, it is headed by General Motors, with $7.145 *billion* of what the government calls "unfunded guaranteed liability." Following them are Chrysler, which is $3.328 billion short; LTV with $3.183 billion; Bethlehem Steel with $1.301 billion; Westinghouse Electric, $692 million; American National Can, $429 million; and scores of top American firms, all of whom represent a potential loss to the American taxpayer if anything should happen to their businesses.

How do they get away with paying out big dividends and giant executive salaries without first fulfilling their government-insured pension obligations to workers?

"Companies can manage to under-fund their pensions in several ways," says a government spokesman. "They can lower their supposed liability by using interest rates beneficial to themselves. Or if they have financial problems, they can get a waiver and not contribute to their pension fund for a few years."

Waivers? The result is that if they go belly-up after they have "waived" their payments for a few years, the pension money is just not there, and Joe Q. Citizen will be stuck with the bill.

What can we do to keep this from being another S&L debacle?

The answer, quite simply, is for Washington to make it illegal for corporations to under-fund pension plans or borrow from them. The corporations should be required to pay their pension costs every year and keep their funds up to date. If they claim they can't afford to make a payment, they should be forced to first eliminate their dividends and reduce their executive overhead.

When the PBGC started in 1974, nobody expected the taxpayers might one day be called upon to support multi-billion-dollar corporations. Someone in Washington is obviously not minding the store.

We used to say that as goes General Motors, so goes the nation. Let's hope that doesn't apply to the trillions at risk in Uncle Sam's guarantee to pay everyone's pension—no matter what.

51

PENSIONS, FEDERAL EMPLOYEES

Royal Retirees

MR. JOHN Q. BUREAUCRAT IS retiring from the federal government in 1993 with a broad grin spread across his face.

Why not? He's had a nice career, ending his days as a GS-15, a specialist rank just below the top executive levels. His salary in his last year was $85,000. He's only fifty-five, but he's put in 30 years, coming to Washington not long after graduating from the University of Michigan.

How will he live now that he's retired?

Very well. He has a new job for the next ten years until he's sixty-five, the usual retirement age, at a nonprofit organization in Washington. It's not as good as his old government position, but he'll get $55,000 a year.

How large a pension will he get from Uncle Sam? Well, that's why he's smiling.

His pension, like that of most federal retirees, will be—according to a government retirement expert—approximately 70% of the highest of his last three years' pay. For Mr. J. Bureaucrat that will be $56,100 a year, a number that will automatically rise each year with the cost-of-living adjustment. So, assuming only a 3.5% inflation rate, ten years after his retirement he will be receiving as much from the taxpayers as when he was working for the government. A pension of $85,000? Absolutely.

How did it get there, and how can we possibly afford it?

In 1984, the government started a new pension system, surely the richest in America. It's called FERS, Federal Employee Retirement System, and it's a triple-threat scheme.

Part I is called a "Defined Benefit." Mr. Bureaucrat contributes less than 1% of his salary, or $680 his last year of employment. To that, over the period of his career, the government will add more than *twenty* times as much.

Part II is Social Security, same as we all pay. He contributes 6.2% of his salary (Medicare is separate), and the government adds the same.

Part III is an investment plan—in stocks, bonds, or government securities—to which he can contribute 5% of his salary. The government will match it dollar for dollar. Even if he decides to contribute nothing, Uncle Sam will pitch in 1% free of charge.

In all, the federal employee is putting in 12% of his gross paycheck if he takes full advantage of the plan. But the generous government is adding an additional 26.4% of his salary each year for his retirement. For the person making $85,000, it means a yearly taxpayer contribution of *$22,440* to his retirement account.

In fact, the ratio of government subsidy is much higher for people who don't take advantage of the 5% investment scheme. Then the retiree puts in only 7%, and the government still adds 21.4%, or three times as much.

But, we might comment, the fifty-five-year-old retiree is still too young to receive his Social Security benefit. Isn't he? Wrong. The government pays him a shadow "Special Social Security Supplement" from its coffers from the time he's fifty-five until he's sixty-two, just as if he were older!

So, in the case of John Q. Bureaucrat, he'll receive his $56,100 pension from the government, get $55,000 more from his job, then truly retire at age sixty-five. By then, his federal pension will have risen (COLAS) to his $85,000 salary, *and* he'll have a new pension from his second job, what is known in the trade as "double dipping." By the time he's sixty-five, his combined pensions will be well over $100,000 a year.

How much will Mr. Bureaucrat cost Uncle Sam in his retirement? Today, a man of fifty-five has a life expectancy of twenty-three years. Beginning with his $56,100 pension in 1993, and ending with his death in 2017, when his pension will have risen to $130,000 a year, the total cost of the retirement payout will be over *$2 million*, or $2,230,000 to be exact. (However, if the retiree is Mrs. Mildred Bureaucrat, who will live an additional four and a half years, the payout will be a half million dollars more.)

Let's also take the case of a non-executive, a GS-10 who began as a GS-2 file clerk, and has risen to become secretary to a top officer, with a salary of $40,000 during her last year. She will retire at fifty-five with a pension of $28,000 and a total payout of $1.7 million.

This year, retirement benefits for civilian government employees will cost $35 billion, plus another $22 billion for military people. (See MILITARY PENSIONS.) That's a lot of money, but it's slated to get much worse.

The government's unfunded pension liability for federal employees is already $1.4 trillion. By the year 2000, the pension payout will be $80 billion a year and the liability up in the $3 trillion range. And that's only the beginning.

What can be done?

Obviously the government has to stop this massive hemorrhaging by reducing the pension benefits by at least 30%, and returning the federal employees to the less-than-perfect world inhabited by the rest of us. That will save us $10 billion a year.

Oh, yes. Forget about that business of paying out Social Security benefits to government workers at age fifty-five. That's just not nice.

52

PENTAGON

Smile, Mr. Parkinson, Smile

BRITISH AUTHOR C. Northcote Parkinson, who invented Parkinson's Law, is no longer young, but his brilliant formulation—which showed how the British Admiralty grew in size as the British Navy disarmed after World War I—is quite alive and kicking.

Here in America, we are seeing it come true again, in another military setting.

This time it's the Pentagon building itself, right across the Potomac from Washington. America is in the midst of the greatest military downsizing since World War II. Aircraft carriers are being mothballed. The Air Force is cutting its combat squadrons in half. Service personnel ranks are being sliced by 25% and probably more.

But in the five-sided headquarters of the Department of Defense, they are unaware of, or immune to, world affairs. Major activity is under way for a large building *expansion*, a thought that would surely bring a grin to Mr. Parkinson's face, wherever he is.

The Pentagon, which now houses 25,000 defense workers, says it urgently needs room for several thousand more people and has convinced Congress to authorize the building of another wing.

"The project will cost $112 million," says a Pentagon

spokesman. "It will increase our office space by some 500,000 square feet. We are taking out some light industry uses—electrical, carpentry, et cetera—and putting in office space, then moving the industrial uses to the new wing. Congress is reexamining the plan, and our people have just testified before several committees, but we expect the expansion to go through."

We do, too.

What is it that Mr. Parkinson knew that we didn't? He thought he was writing about the British Admiralty, but he obviously had a firm understanding of the American federal government as well.

As Parkinson has taught us, the smaller the function, the greater the management. The more the shrinkage of mission, the larger the expansion of bureaucracy.

At the Pentagon, we are seeing his vision come true before our eyes. And it won't cost us any $112 million as the spokesman claims. If it's a penny, it'll be at least a quarter billion. That is, if Mr. Parkinson stays the seer history has proven him to be.

53

PORK BARREL

For the Folks Back Home

THE OLDEST ADAGE in Washington is that "all politics are local."

Congressmen never forget it, and while one eye may be focused on the national commonweal, at least one other is zeroed in on what can be wangled for the folks back home, the people he hopes will reelect him next November.

The amendment, private bill, twisted appropriation—however he can manage it—becomes the obsession of many a Congressman. His life seems dominated by how much in "pork barrel" gifts for his constituents he can get through the House or Senate. Sometimes the present is only for a private corporation, a university, or even a single individual. But the theory is that it brings "federal money" into the district and keeps it from going somewhere else.

These gifts serve not only a local function, but are like political trading stamps for the Congressman. He supports his colleagues' whims in order to later receive the same consideration.

A President can also play this lowest of political games. During a primary or general election, he can suddenly dispense free-floating federal funds to certain states or districts to beef up the campaign of Congressmen and Senators of his own party. Or he can even use the trick during his own primary or reelection bid.

The term "pork barrel" stems back to the early 1800s when the popular meat was packed that way, and hungry farm hands reached in for slabs of salt pork. In 1879, it was adopted as political slang to mean goodies for the local district paid for by the taxpayers at large. Over the years, tales of unique pork (as it's now inelegantly termed) gave citizens a temporary smile, as they still do. But as time goes on, the expensive practice has become such an addiction that it's now more fiscally tragic than funny.

In this section, we'd like to take a moment to list what we believe is the most extensive record of pork-barrel legislation ever printed—a compendium gathered from dozens of sources: government, foundations, libraries, and members of Congress themselves. These items are not listed alphabetically, or in any logical order, but for the record, here goes:

- A $60,000 Belgian endive research study for the University of Massachusetts.
- $6.4 million for a Bavarian ski resort in Kellogg, Idaho.
- $13 million to repair a privately owned dam in South Carolina.
- $3.1 million to convert a ferry boat into a crab restaurant in Baltimore.
- $43 million for Steamtrain, U.S.A., in Scranton, Pennsylvania, to recreate a railroad yard of old.
- $107,000 to study the sex life of the Japanese quail.
- $4.3 million for a privately owned museum in Johnstown, Pennsylvania.

- $11 million for a private pleasure boat harbor in Cleveland.
- $150,000 to study the Hatfield-McCoy feud.
- $6 million to repair tracks owned by the Soo Railroad Line.
- $320,000 to purchase President McKinley's mother-in-law's house.
- Funds to rehabilitate the South Carolina mansion of Charles Pickney, a Framer of the Constitution. Unfortunately, the house was built after he died.
- $2.7 million for a catfish farm in Arkansas.
- $84,000 to find out why people fall in love.
- $1 million to study why people don't ride bikes to work.
- $19 million to examine gas emissions from cow flatulence.
- $3 million for private parking garages in Chicago.
- $1.8 million for topographic maps of two parishes in Louisiana.
- $144,000 to see if pigeons follow human economic laws.
- Funds to study the cause of rudeness on tennis courts and examine smiling patterns in bowling alleys.
- $219,000 to teach college students how to watch television.
- $500,000 to build a replica of the Great Pyramid of Egypt in Indiana.
- $850,000 for a bicycle path in Macomb County, Michigan.
- $10 million for an access ramp in a privately owned stadium in Milwaukee.
- $1.8 million for an engineering study to convert Biscayne Boulevard in Miami into an "exotic garden."

- $13 million for an industrial theme park in Pennsylvania.
- $500,000 for a museum to honor former Secretary of State Cordell Hull.
- $2 million to construct an ancient Hawaiian canoe.
- $350,000 to renovate the House Beauty Salon.
- $6 million to upgrade the two-block-long Senate subway.
- $20 million for a demonstration project to build wooden bridges.
- $160,000 to study if you can hex an opponent by drawing an X on his chest.
- $250,000 to study TV lighting in the Senate meeting rooms.
- $800,000 for a restroom on Mt. McKinley.
- $100,000 to study how to avoid falling spacecraft.
- $100,000 to research soybean-based ink.
- $1 million for a Seafood Consumer Center.
- $130,000 for a Congressional video-conferencing project.
- $16,000 to study the operation of the *komungo*, a Korean stringed instrument.
- $1 million to preserve a Trenton, New Jersey, sewer as a historic monument.
- $6000 for a document on Worcestershire sauce.
- $10,000 to study the effect of naval communications on a bull's potency.
- $33 million to pump sand onto the private beaches of Miami hotels.
- $10 million to a small Pennsylvania college to study separation stress in military families.
- $57,000 spent by the Executive Branch for gold-embossed playing cards on Air Force Two.

The saddest commentary on this irresponsible extravagance came from former Senator William Proxmire of Wisconsin.

"I have spent my career trying to get Congressmen to spend the people's money as if it were their own," he said on leaving the Senate. "But I have failed."

Nothing says more about the insensitivity of the U.S. Congress than its pork appropriations. They are imaginative, have a touch of whimsy, and are of little or no national value.

But they are an opportunity to spend a great deal of money, the mother's milk of the modern federal establishment.

54

PORK, WEST VIRGINIA STYLE

He Moves Governments

THERE HAVE BEEN legislative masters of pork legislation over the years, influential Congressmen on Ways and Means, or Appropriations, who hated to see a bill pass through their hands without tacking on a gift for the folks back home.

But the sobriquet of "Prince of Pork" truly belongs to a contemporary Senator, Robert Byrd of West Virginia, former Majority Leader of that body, and now Chairman of the powerful Senate Appropriations Committee.

Other Senators are content to wangle $20–30 million of bequests for their states, a series of small projects for a bridge here, a road there, a university building or two. Back home, they parade their pork like crusaders' banners and get appropriate kudos.

Oh, Byrd does the same. He recently played the traditional game by getting $4.5 million of federal money to renovate the Keith-Albee movie house in Huntington, West Virginia, as a symbol of the "old Hollywood." The cinema coup was only one of dozens of pork products he has brought home to his state.

But his true skill is unprecedented: Senator Byrd has decided to move major units of the federal government from the glamorous banks of the Potomac and bring them to the dowdy hills of West Virginia, complete and intact. And he's doing it.

We're not just talking small, obscure sub-agencies that he can make look like major coups. No, the Prince of Pork needn't brag. He is moving *large* pieces of Washington—lock, stock, and deficit—down home to West Virginia. And as Chairman of Senate Appropriations, he has more power than the President in making his wishes stick. Otherwise, many of the White House's pet projects could find themselves stuck in the bureaucracy of Byrd's committee staff.

Byrd's first coup was bringing the Coast Guard's national Computer Operations Center to land-locked Martinsburg, West Virginia. After that he followed up with a NASA research center in Wheeling.

But these efforts pale before his most recent acquisition for the Mountain State, which was a big one. The FBI Identification Unit, where 190 million fingerprints are stored, was happily ensconced in the luxurious Beltway atmosphere. But where are they now?

The short, natty Senator, addicted to non-matching vests, who for years ran the Democratic Party in the Senate, has moved them to Clarksburg, West Virginia, a small town of 18,000 some four hours by car from the Potomac. The FBI building, which is now under construction, will cost taxpayers $185 million and will house 2800 employees.

But Byrd is not finished. He is now in a competitive battle with the state of Virginia, and with CIA Director Robert Gates, in a fight to take a good hunk of the CIA from some two dozen of its locations in the sophisticated Washington area—a fit environment for American 007s—and ship almost 3000 of them to Charles Town, a rural village in the West Virginia hills. The cost of this project is now up to $1.4 billion, and Gates is desperately fighting the move, having just temporarily "suspended" what looked like a done deal.

But history shows that in the final analysis nobody in Washington messes with Mr. Byrd. The President may chide some of his Cabinet people when they misbehave, but this wily Chairman of the Senate Appropriations Committee can do much more: he can banish them, and their agency, to the hinterlands of West Virginia.

That, my friends, is real pork.

55

POST OFFICES

Small and Expensive

THIS IS no time to discuss the inefficiencies of the U.S. Postal Service. That would require volumes.

But it might be worthwhile to indulge in a touch of nostalgia, back to the time in the 1940s when people received two mail deliveries a day and stamps cost three cents. (Some remember three deliveries in New York City!) That all came to an abrupt halt in 1950, when once a day became the rule.

The Post Office doesn't like to be reminded about that era of the swift-of-foot. But there is one touch of nostalgia they stick with faithfully. It is the traditional, tiny rural post offices that do not deliver mail, and sometimes serve only a handful of people. Closing them could save as much as $150 million a year.

No one wants to keep our country cousins out of the postal system. Quite the opposite. Right now, it is the *customers* who have to brave the rain and sleet and darkness to pick up their own mail. If these small offices were closed, they would get rural free delivery at a fraction of the present cost.

Are there many of these outdated, expensive, miniature facilities?

Yes, thousands. The number of post offices has been

declining since 1900, when there were 70,000 in the nation. The system grew from Colonial times along with the population and the realities of political patronage. Every post office meant another Postmaster anointed by the President as a reward for political loyalty.

Today, as postal patronage has disappeared (with the reorganization in 1971) and as shipment of mail has been modernized, we are down to 35,000 facilities. Of these, at last count, some 8000 were too small to deliver mail. In fact, 3300 of them served fewer than 100 people. Another 2000 post offices had fewer than 200 customers. Some even served fewer than 10 families!

The economics of the small post office are all wrong. In a typical case, in a rural Eastern town, the office served 115 customers in general delivery or postal boxes. The post office had a full-time Postmaster and a part-time helper. Revenue was $7,740, but expenses were $25,256—quite a loss on the national level.

"We could easily save $100–150 million a year by closing them all down," says a government auditor of the Postal Service. "But you have to realize that these small post offices have social value. It's a place where neighbors meet. It has a sense of nostalgia."

True, but there are other nostalgic images as well. Like the time carriers used to make two deliveries a day, and our nation had a balanced budget.

56

PRESIDENTIAL ELECTIONS

We Pay for the Air Pollution

"MY OPPONENT IS a fake, a bum, a liar, an elitist. And besides, he inhales."

We sit by our television sets during the Presidential campaigns, mesmerized by negative commercials conjured up by what used to be called "hucksters," advertising agencies who are paid to refocus our frustrations away from their candidate and onto the other guy.

We say "tsk, tsk," as if we are not involved in this pollution of our airwaves by the lowest denominator of any political operation since the heyday of Tammany Hall (Democrats) and Teapot Dome (Republicans).

In reality, it is we, the taxpayers, through our $1 contributions on IRS forms, who pay for most of the Presidential race, including those noxious commercials. From that source, the Federal Election Commission will take in enough money to spend at least $200 million on the Chief Executive cockfight.

Americans believe that most campaign funds come from contributors, including fat cats. That's not true. Once the candidates have been chosen at the conventions, the fall Presidential campaign is financed—100%—by public money. So, sadly, those political television ads are self-inflicted—paid for by us in perhaps the greatest misuse of public funds on record.

In the fall of 1992, for example, the FEC will dispense $55 million of our money to each of the two major candidates to spend as they see fit. In fact, they can't spend any additional funds of their own. We, the people, pay for the entire sweepstakes, but we have no control over the rules of the engagement. At least not yet.

We may also laugh at the hijinks on the floor of the Democratic and Republican conventions. But again, it is our doing. Each major party receives $11 million from Uncle Sam for its Presidential conventions. The only funds the Democrats and Republicans are allowed to spend at their own shindigs are for whooping it up.

In fact, it is only during the primaries—when the FEC matches *individual* contributions of up to $250—that candidates can directly dispense money they've raised from PACs and voters. The maximum a candidate could spend in the 1992 primaries was $27 million, half of which came from the FEC kitty.

In essence, the Presidential race is a citizen-supported pageant. We have little to say about its decorum, but we may be called upon to put up still more money, this time from the depleted Treasury.

"We're running out of funds," says a spokesman for the Federal Election Commission. "We expect a shortfall of $75–100 million for the 1996 election."

If Congress wants things to stay as they are, they'll have to appropriate the difference. But that shortfall will also enable voters to shout their opinion.

What can we do? Several simple things will change the face of American presidential politics.

(1) We should badger our members of Congress to require that candidates who take public funds *eliminate* all negative political advertising from their campaigns.

(2) Take the final—truly radical, truly cleansing, to-

tally legal—step. Just as the Congress years ago instructed the Federal Communications Commission to stop all liquor and cigarette ads on television and radio, let's do the same with politics. Let's outlaw *all television and radio political ads*, relying instead on free televised debates and other traditional campaign methods.

(3) Reduce the size of Presidential campaigns, returning to an era of debates, stump speeches, walk-through handshakes, and free media space and time. Put a cap on the cost of future Presidential campaigns and severely limit the size of contributions to candidates and political parties. (See Conclusion for details.)

With the elimination of television advertising, the scale of the mad quadrennial sweepstakes will become saner. Maybe then the people can come back into the act, as supporters and perhaps even as candidates.

Not only will it clean up the pollution of politics, but taxpayers will save millions, which can then be used to reduce the federal deficit.

Ever been to an old-fashioned whistle-stop?

57

PRINTING

Anyone for Monopoly?

WASHINGTON LIKES to pretend it knows something about business, but whenever it gets involved, it falls on its fiscal face.

A case in point is the printing bill of the government, which runs more than $1 billion a year. Everyone agrees that it's way too much, but no one does anything about it.

One major reason the cost is so high is that the government decided to go into the printing business 130 years ago, which was a strategic error. As a result, the Government Printing Office, which handles the enormous job of turning out billions of pages of laws and reports, has a monopoly on the business, with the extra costs that automatically creates.

"MONOPOLY-LIKE STATUS CONTRIBUTES TO INEFFICIENCY AND INEFFECTIVENESS," headlined a recent government audit of the GPO. But despite this and other attacks, the agency energetically resists real reform.

The Government Printing Office started life on the first day of Lincoln's Administration in 1861, some say in order to get the *Congressional Record* printed overnight, which was then difficult in Washington. Today, there are dozens of firms who could do the job, cheaper and better.

"GPO's monopoly-like role in providing government printing services was created to assure efficiency," says the report on the 5000-employee organization. "But with the passage of time that role has been transformed; it now perpetuates inefficiency because centralized control permits the GPO to be insulated from market forces."

Of its billion dollars in business, $150 million is printed in government-owned and -operated plants near the Capitol. The same work, says the audit, could have "been procured from commercial printers for as little as $75 million," a savings of half. Others believe the price would be even less.

The agency itself reports that its printing and binding machines were idle 53% of the time during the regular work week. Despite this, they scheduled a "significant amount of work on weekends," with overtime pay, the auditors concluded. The GPO's paper waste was also shown to be considerably higher than that of others in the industry, and its printing quality lower.

Is there an answer to the problem?

Yes. Simply close it down and get the government out of the business. Uncle Sam could take his $1 billion printing budget, which should be cut by $250 million anyway, and contract the work to private printing companies all over the nation.

The result: a fortune saved in taxpayer funds, and a lesson to Washington to mind its own business—whatever that is.

58

PUBLIC RELATIONS

Army of Flacks

LIKE PRIVATE INDUSTRY, the federal government has its "image merchants," publicists straining mightily to put the best possible face on the Washington operation.

Americans may be suspicious of government excess, but they lack knowledge of what's really happening behind the scenes. Credit, or discredit, for much of this goes to the public-relations specialists who work in the Public Affairs offices of federal agencies, from the White House (39 people) to a small air base in Texas (1 person).

Their job is to influence the media, and through them, the voters on the glories of (1) the administration in power, of whatever party; (2) the particular federal agency, whether NASA or the Department of Transportation, so that they can procure larger appropriations from Congress; (3) their boss, the Cabinet or sub-Cabinet-level employer, who's almost always a political appointee.

An unspoken part of the PR person's job is to keep the media from learning, or even inquiring about, the enormous waste in government. In this area, they have done a near-perfect job.

Are there a few score, or even a few hundred, of what used to be called "flacks" working for Uncle Sam?

The Office of Personnel Management, which has figures on all government specialists, reports (and it's still hard to believe) that there are *4000* publicists presenting the federal apparatus in the best possible light. That's about four times as many editorial people as work for the *New York Times* worldwide.

Washington's public-relations army is an expensive one. Most PR people fall in the GS-11 to GS-15 range, with maximum salaries of $42,000 to $84,000. Along with their compensation and benefits, the cost of secretaries and support people, plus office costs and overhead, we're talking about a billion dollars a year.

The cost is particularly galling because their efforts have kept Citizen Doe from learning the truth about Washington and acting on it. (One caveat to this criticism: *if* you know what questions to ask, you can break through the wall of silence. Federal PR people are helpful and polite, if evasive.)

The solution?

Cut the PR ranks in half right away, then look at them again a year later. The savings will be at least a half billion dollars.

If the United States government is doing a good job—which it isn't—the people will be the first to know about it, without the help of federal publicists.

59

RESEARCH, UNIVERSITIES

Let's Party on Uncle Sam!

THE UNIVERSITY RESEARCHER was pleased that his $250,000 federal grant to study the genetic causes of schizophrenia had come through from the National Institutes of Health. It was one of the thousands of such scientific grants that cost taxpayers $9 billion in 1992.

His government funds were virtually spent the moment he received them—for staff and equipment. The professor was lucky if he finished his work before the money ran out.

But back at the university headquarters, they were virtually panting over the luxuries *their* large piece of the federal cash would buy. Along with the professor's grant, the university received a check for $200,000 from the NIH for the "indirect costs" of handling the research.

What could they do with it?

There was a trip to Berlin for the university president; a driver for his wife's limousine; fresh flowers daily in the Dean's office; renovation of the competition basketball court; and a giant homecoming reception for the class of 1972, including a gown for the one-time Campus Queen, a six-piece rock group, and all the booze the college officials and alumni could down in six hours of revelry.

All, of course, courtesy of the American taxpayer.

Is this opening anecdote fictional? Yes. But is it an exaggeration? Probably not, as we shall see.

Each year, as part of the $9 billion spent on university-based health and science research, $3 billion goes directly to schools for supposedly legitimate and "allowable" overhead. But today, as audits of 61 leading research universities are being conducted by the Inspector General of Health and Human Services, the Defense Department, and the General Accounting Office, word of possible abuse is emerging.

The investigations reveal that the waste depicted in the anecdote above may be an understatement of the facts. There is not just one isolated campus scandal. Partying and high living on the taxpayer's nickel are becoming commonplace at some of our top research universities.

The investigation began with the charges of Mr. Paul Biddle, a Navy Contracting Officer at Stanford University, who was originally shouted down by both the Navy and the school. But he persevered, and the inquiry has since spread to include hearings held by Congressman John Dingell, Chairman of the Committee on Energy and Commerce.

When the inquiry was completed, investigators found that the following universities had allegedly billed these unallowable "indirect costs" to the government. We'll start with the most publicized case, that of Stanford University.

STANFORD UNIVERSITY

- Depreciation on the school's 72-foot yacht, *Victoria*
- $6000 for cedar-lined closets in the president's home
- $2000 a month for fresh-cut flowers
- $1000 a month for laundry bills

- $1500 for liquor at pre-football-game parties
- Money to enlarge the president's bed
- $7000 for sheets for the enlarged bed
- $45,000 for a "retreat" for Stanford trustees at Lake Tahoe
- Two Voltaire chairs at $1500 each
- $33,000 annual dues to the American Association of Universities
- $185,000 administrative expenses for a shopping center owned by the university
- $12,000 for student activities, including a Fraternity Task Force
- $64,000 toward the upkeep of the chancellor's residence, even though he had died five years before
- $2072 toward student dances, soft drinks, bands, movie rentals, and a beach trip
- $525,000 for computer systems to raise funds
- $249,000 for parking-lot expenses
- Monies toward the cost of a reception welcoming the president's wife to Stanford

Over the last ten years, Stanford has received $1.8 *billion* from the government, of which about $700 million were in "indirect costs." Biddle claims that Stanford, which initially flatly denied owning a yacht, could owe the government some $200 million. Stanford has revealed that government grants pay for a quarter of Stanford's entire budget.

DARTMOUTH COLLEGE

- The costs of defending an anti-trust suit
- Miscellaneous real estate
- Cost of publishing Daniel Webster's papers

- Senior society anniversary celebration
- Administrative sabbatical
- Library maintenance
- Liquor

YALE UNIVERSITY

- Student financial aid audit by CPA
- Flowers
- Memorial service for a past president
- Gifts
- Artwork given as gifts
- President's travel
- Housing expenses for university officers

HARVARD MEDICAL SCHOOL

- Money for athletic facilities
- Recruiting new faculty member, including paying the points and mortgage on his condominium

MASSACHUSETTS INSTITUTE OF TECHNOLOGY

- Catered parties and receptions
- Trips to the Caribbean
- Artwork
- Floral designs

RUTGERS UNIVERSITY

- $5.5 million in unallowable funds (voluntarily withdrawn by the university)

JOHNS HOPKINS UNIVERSITY

- President's trip to Europe
- Social club dues
- Liquor
- Catered affairs and parties

UNIVERSITY OF PITTSBURGH

- Leased car, driver, mobile phone for president
- Christmas cards
- Trip to Cayman Islands for president's wife
- Trip to Dublin, Ireland, for soccer match
- Liquor
- Golf club membership
- Rental of aircraft
- French language lessons

DUKE UNIVERSITY

- Art museum expenses
- Stretch limo services
- Receptions
- Founder's Day expenses
- Faculty dinner and dance gifts
- Country club membership dues

EMORY UNIVERSITY

- Membership dues for social clubs
- Liquor for a party
- Storyteller for Christmas function

TEXAS SOUTHWESTERN MEDICAL CENTER

- Dinner party
- Valet parking
- 10 engraved crystal decanters
- Engraved cocktail napkins

WASHINGTON UNIVERSITY, ST. LOUIS

- Severance pay for a tenured professor
- Piece of sculpture
- Preparing a history of the school
- Inappropriate housing costs
- Parties

UNIVERSITY OF SOUTHERN CALIFORNIA

- Trustee conferences
- Student newspaper
- University communications
- News service
- Faculty senate
- Presidential search and transition

The "indirect costs," which have now eaten up some $30 billion of Treasury money, seem to have provided conservative universities with a slush fund of temptation normally not available to academic people.

It all began in 1947 when the government decided to back up research grants with partial reimbursement of school overhead. The first subsidy was a flat 8% of the research grant, which rose to 15% in the early 1950s, and again to 20% in 1963.

Over the years, the "indirect" gimmick kept increasing. From 20% it rose to 30, 40, 50%, and more. Best estimates show that these loose subsidies are now equal to 52% of the actual health and science grants. But some schools get considerably more, citing their prestige and operating expenses. Stanford was one of the highest with 72%, while Harvard Medical School and Columbia University were even higher.

As a result of the investigation, Stanford has been cut back to the average 52% overhead, which will save the government $28 million a year. But thus far the other alleged violators have not been affected at all.

What can we do to continue the research program yet curb universities gone wild at the prospect of free government money?

This might be a reasonable course of action:

(1) Make it illegal for any tax money to be used by universities for personal purposes, travel, parties, liquor, purchase of furniture and antiques, flowers, or receptions.

(2) Cut the $3 billion subsidy in half. This will provide an immediate saving of $1.5 billion, and a tempering influence on academic people who have lost their philosophical footing.

(3) Do no further negotiating of the amount with universities. Set the overhead allowance at 25% for all schools, with no exceptions.

(4) Make a yearly spot audit of a dozen or so schools at random.

The saving will be twofold: reduction in the deficit, and redemption of a once-upstanding community overcome by greed.

Did they say $7000 for bed sheets?

60

RURAL ELECTRIFICATION AND TELEPHONES

Hang Up and Run

WHEN ONE RAILS about "special interests," there's no better target than the Rural Electrification Administration, or REA.

Created in 1935 when only 10% of rural America had electricity, it was one of the stellar successes of the New Deal. The government loaned money to small electric cooperatives at 2% interest, which was then the going rate. By 1952, 90% of rural America had already been electrified. By the 1960s, the figure had reached 98%, and by the 1970s, 99% of the rural nation was on line.

Having achieved victory, did the REA fold its bureaucratic tents? Quite the opposite. Following Parkinson's Law, they expanded their operation when there was little left to do. In the last twenty years, the agency has been a model of waste—spending massive sums that were not, and are not, needed by farms that are as well lit as the Great White Way.

The REA is still loaning out money, this time at far below market interest rates, and losing a fortune in the process. They have spawned 1000 utility co-ops, many of which are inefficient and, admits the REA, need to be merged into larger units. In fact, many REA beneficiaries are no longer "rural," as the interstate highways have brought the suburbs out to meet them.

To date, the REA has loaned out and guaranteed $63 billion, with $36 billion still outstanding. Beginning in 1952, the government started losing money on their low-interest rates, and the program turned into a subsidy. Almost a half century after it started, it's still charging its borrowers—many of whom are well established—only 5% interest. This is at a time when the government is paying 8% for its money. In fact, during the 1970s and 1980s, the REA had to pay up to 12% for cash, but still funneled it to REA borrowers for 5%.

Let's look at the most recent scorecard of the REA, and its junior partner, the Rural Telephone Bank—established in 1949 and now with 5 million customers.

In 1991, new REA loans totaled $1.7 billion. Their balance sheet shows the sad result. The bureaucracy cost $33 million to run, but that was only a minuscule part of the charge to taxpayers. The interest subsidy was $239 million plus another $494 million provision for losses on several shaky loans. The subtotal? Almost three quarter *billion* dollars for homes that were electrified 30 and 40 years ago.

A new scandal has just surfaced, this time at the Rural Telephone Bank. It involves giant utilities who are using an REA loophole to suck the taxpayer dry. Most of the Bank's telephone borrowers are private companies who've been making money and have even branched out into the cellular business. They've become ripe takeovers for giants like GTE and Alltel, who after absorbing them, tap into their access to cheap REA money.

The mammoth telephone holding companies have already borrowed a *billion* dollars from the taxpayers at the

5% cut-rate interest, a loss of an extra $40 million a year for the Treasury. In fact, because they can get their REA applications in early—in an agency that deals in "first come, first served"—they've received the lion's share of the available loans, pushing out the mom-and-pop operations.

The REA is a federal dinosaur. It still exists only because of rural Congressmen who want to satisfy their special-interest constituency—at the taxpayer's expense.

The solution?

Close down the REA. Stop all future loans. Raise the interest rate on the outstanding money. Call the loans to big utilities, and get the money back. Hold on to a handful of people to collect the interest on the $36 billion outstanding, and try to recoup the principal.

In political history, the REA will be recorded as a rarity, a government project that worked—*until* it outlived its usefulness by a generation.

61

SMALL BUSINESS ADMINISTRATION

So Much for So Few

LET'S SAY you're a painting contractor with a crew of four, and you're facing hard times because of a slump in the housing industry. Can you apply to the government's Small Business Administration for a federally guaranteed loan to tide you over until better times?

You can apply, but it won't do you any good. Uncle Sam's definition of a small business is a hell of lot different from yours and mine. A recent study of loans granted by the SBA showed the typical firm involved grossed approximately a million dollars a year.

"Businesses with revenues of $3.5 million, and in certain cases up to $14.5 million, may be considered small depending on the type of product they offer," flatly states a government report on the SBA.

But they will help you out if you have a very good cash flow, which means you don't need them. Who qualifies for this largesse? Well, some of their favorite clients in that category are your poor neighborhood doctor, dentist, lawyer, accountant—well-to-do professionals who are increasingly supported by the federal Treasury and your pocketbook through the SBA.

An SBA computer readout, especially done for this writer, shows that in 1990 and 1991, the SBA gave out 2092 loans to professionals, from doctors to management consultants, for a total of almost a *half billion* dollars.

There are an estimated 15 million small businesses in America, most of which are operating on slippery ground. With the slightest shove, they can fall—as they do increasingly—into the abyss of bankruptcy.

Is the SBA there to help them? Think again. We're generally talking *big* business at the Small Business Administration. They can guarantee up to $750,000 of a loan (which might total over a million dollars) to firms with net worth up to $6 million, some of whom have had assets of over $20 million and as many as 1500 employees.

How many companies are helped out yearly and what does it cost the taxpayer?

The answers, in shorthand, are "few" and "a lot of money."

This past year, the SBA made or guaranteed loans to a minuscule percentage of small businesses—23,000 to be exact—at an enormous taxpayer cost of $837 million. That's quite a price for the handful helped.

And what about losses? Is the default rate high?

Of the $10 billion now out in loans, we can expect large losses if history is any guide. In 1990 alone, the government had to eat $1.1 billion in liquidations. Nonperforming loans reached a peak of 28% in 1983, and have since dropped somewhat, but are still at a huge 16%, which would bankrupt any bank. The difference is that the SBA bank is backed by "the full faith and credit of the United States Government," which means you and me. One category, "energy loans," has had a 36% default rate.

What should be done?

Unless we can come up with a scheme to help large

numbers of really small businesses, which would probably be too expensive, we should close down the elite Small Business Administration. As it now stands it is just another federal boondoggle for a few people—and not usually the right ones—at the expense of us all.

Savings? Almost a billion dollars a year. And that's not so "small."

62

SOCIAL SECURITY

How to Cheat the Aged

THE GREAT UNRESOLVED GOVERNMENT SCANDAL of our time is the abuse of the Social Security taxes—plus the misuse of that money over the years—by the Congress and the President.

Today, that abuse has become endemic. In 1992, the government will "borrow"—a euphemism for "steal"—$50 billion from the Social Security fund and use it to pay the general bills of its bloated bureaucracy.

That's not a one-year aberration. It's been going on for some time, and the Social Security fund now has government IOUs for *$330 billion*. In no time, the government will have taken $1 trillion from the aged, money that could, and should, be used to increase benefits or lower Social Security taxes.

The problem started in 1935 when FDR put through the Federal Old Age Insurance and Survivors Act, which set up the system. It was called the Social Security Trust Fund, but that's only rhetoric. The money was never really segregated, or in trust, and the government constantly borrowed from it.

Where did all this recent surplus money come from? In 1983, Congress and the President, seeking to "save" the system, raised Social Security taxes, creating an enormous pool of money. It's estimated that there will be a $6 *trillion* surplus by the year 2030. But will the money really be there? Not if the profligate federal government continues to take it, as they're now doing.

Washington is playing a nasty shell game with the aged citizens' money. By using this surplus as part of the general fund instead of borrowing money on the outside, they can pretend that the deficit is smaller than it really is. A true accounting in 1992 would show a $450 billion deficit instead of the $400 billion claimed.

Ironically, the people's Social Security money is being used to help pay the retirement pensions of federal employees, which are much richer than those of the average citizen. (SEE PENSIONS, FEDERAL EMPLOYEES.)

Senator Daniel Moynihan of New York proposed exposing this sham by suggesting the government lower Social Security taxes, but politicians of both parties, knowing that much of the government is living off the aged, howled him down.

Today a majority of all people pay more in Social Security taxes than they do in regular income taxes, a percentage that increases each year. In fact, Social Security is the vehicle for a secret yearly tax increase for Americans of all ages.

In 1991, the maximum base for the Social Security tax (7.65% for employees and 15.3% for the self-employed) was $53,400. In 1992, that was raised to $55,000, based on a supposed increase in the average wage. But that was before inflation. Income taxes are "indexed" for inflation, but Social Security taxes are not. So even if a person stands still in real earnings, his retirement taxes go up every year—funneled not into his pension plan, but into the yawning pit of government waste.

If the government didn't cheat its aged, Social Security

taxes, which are too high, could be lowered considerably without affecting benefits. Or the surplus could be invested in such guaranteed bonds as Fannie Maes, starting the Social Security fund on a growth pattern like other pension plans. With increased benefits, retirement could become a true option for many. Instead, today's average payment of $625 a month keeps many sixty-five-year-olds working.

What is the solution?

(1) Social Security was not designed to pay somebody else's bills. Congress needs to pass a law permanently segregating the fund and prohibiting the federal government from borrowing any more of its money.

(2) The $330 billion owed should be paid back in the next few years, with interest.

(3) All future surpluses should be fully invested in government-backed securities, with the proceeds used to either lower Social Security taxes or increase the benefits.

If we had done that 60 years ago, our senior citizens would now be comfortable retirees.

But the least we can do today is to stop cheating our aged.

63

SOCIAL SERVICE CONSOLIDATION

Duplication and Overlap

"DUPLICATION AND OVERLAP" are not a Washington law firm but the theme song of the American federal government, which often performs the same missions in dozens of different agencies in a dozen different ways.

If you were to put the word "children," for example, into a computer of the Office of Management and Budget, you'd come up with scores of programs run by individual agencies, each mobilizing its competitive blood.

The 1993 budget boasts of several programs under the heading "Investing in America's Children," one of the fastest growing categories in the government. It states: "The Budget provides $100 billion for children's programs, up 66% since 1989."

Childhood immunization, for example, has four funding sources: Centers for Disease Control Childhood Immunization Grants, Medicaid EPSDT Screening, Maternal and Child Health Care Block Grant, and Preventive Health Block Grant. As part of the $9 billion program to reduce infant mortality, three major agencies—the Public Health Service, Medicaid, and the Department of Agriculture—are almost equally involved.

The same, as we have seen, is true in job training, where a dozen agencies compete for the same people.

They duplicate as they go, without any central route to reach the unemployed.

Education is on the budget of virtually every agency. In fact, Head Start (pre-schooling for children) is not even an activity of the heavily budgeted Department of Education.

Physical fitness and healthy diets come out of several sources: the FDA; School Health Education Activities, President's Council on Physical Fitness, and the National Institutes of Health Exercise and Fitness Research. (They forgot the Department of Labor's home economics' nutrition program, among others.)

Urban grants are the province of many agencies, including HUD, Health and Human Services, even the Department of Agriculture, which, as we shall see, has moved quietly into the city along with the mountain-based Appalachian Regional Commission.

Environmental protection is split up fully ten ways: from America the Beautiful, a Lady Bird Johnson legacy whose budget of $785 million has more than doubled in three years, to the Superfund to Global Change Research, which went from zero dollars in 1989 to well over a *billion* today. Coastal America is handled by four agencies; wetlands by five.

Some of this wasteful duplication has come to the attention of the Congressional Budget Office, which recently asked for the consolidation of five new childhood programs started since 1989. All operate independently with enormous budgets that total more than $5 billion and range from the "Title IV-A 'At Risk' Child Care" to "Dependent Care Planning and Development Grants."

By consolidating them, says the CBO, "duplicate services could be eliminated, and administrative costs would decline because of simpler rules and regulations plus a reduction in administrative personnel. Moreover, different services provided to the same individual or family could be integrated more easily."

Amen.

What is the answer?

Consolidate all similar activities under a *single* roof.

For example, the CBO says that by putting the five childhood programs under one umbrella, we could save $270 million a year.

Just think what would happen if someone did a "mission analysis" on each program in the federal government, then tried to unravel the overlapping by moving all those with the same objectives into one agency.

Not only would we save billions but—for the very first time—Congress and the President might actually learn what they're buying.

They'd also discover the enormous power of those twins, Duplication and Overlap, in the Washington Establishment.

64

STUDENTS, COLLEGE

Grants, Loans, and to Hell with the Middle Class

THE STUDENT at a New York state college desperately needed a loan. With only the barest essentials, the schooling would cost $6000 a year. His parents, a working-class couple on Long Island, made ends meet on their combined salaries, but after federal, Social Security, state, and burdensome local property taxes, they had no money left to send their son to college.

The young man consulted the school's financial adviser and the local bank about getting a Stafford Student Loan, guaranteed by the government. The decision: they could give him only $1000. His parents ostensibly "made too much" for him to get a meaningful student loan.

"I've lost twenty pounds because I don't get that much to eat anymore," he says.

This year, Uncle Sam is spending a fortune—$13.7 billion—trying to help students get through college. But in typical Washington fashion, the programs are inequitable, poorly thought out, and extraordinarily wasteful.

They do only half the job needed and cost the taxpayer twice as much as they should.

The first inequity is the Pell Grant, which is an outright

gift that costs the taxpayers $6 billion a year. Who gets this grant?

The Department of Education calculates it on the basis of a complex formula involving family assets, income, and, surprisingly, the expected cost of the college. By strange Washington logic, the student going to Harvard has a better chance for a Pell than someone satisfied with a less-expensive state college.

But its greatest inequity is the bias against the hard-pressed middle class. (This new stepchild of the federal government seems to be paying for everyone else, rich and poor alike.) The effective Pell Grant family-income ceiling, for instance, is $29,000. Students who qualify can get $10,000 and more in grants over four years, but a family that earns $30,000—barely enough to live on in some parts of the country—is out of luck.

Washington also ignores regional differences in its typical irrational manner. In Oklahoma, $30,000 goes pretty far. On Long Island, where home prices and property taxes are among the highest in America, it provides only a marginal existence—surely not enough to send a child to college.

(The government is contemplating raising the $29,000 ceiling, but that still leaves out anyone—no matter how hard-pressed—who makes $1 more. It is a *mean* means test.)

The Department of Education provides considerably more to students through the Stafford guaranteed loan program, which now has $57 billion at work. Students pay no interest while in school, then 8% when they start to repay—if they repay—six months after graduation.

Are there that many defaults, or is it just the case of an occasional unconcerned student?

Actually, it's an epidemic. Twenty-nine percent of

those who graduated from college three years ago are now in default, adding to an enormous—and I believe unnecessary—burden on the American taxpayer.

In 1992, the government will pay banks $3.5 billion just for defaulted loans and almost $3 billion in interest subsidies, even though the banks take absolutely no risk.

Is there an answer to both student need and the overstrained national pocketbook?

Absolutely. Here it is:

(1) Offer *all* college students loans of up to $6000 a year, without a means test and without any turn-downs. Twenty-four thousand dollars will take most young people, poor or middle class, through a four-year program at a public university. If they want to go to private colleges and can afford it, they can pay the difference themselves or try to qualify for scholarships.

How can we afford such a program?

Easy.

(2) Drop the Pell Grants entirely, as totally superfluous in this new loan program. Parents may be poor, even unemployed, but the students themselves—once they graduate from college with the help of $24,000 in loans—will have the same ability as anyone else to repay the money. The taxpayer savings, thus far, are $6 billion dollars.

What about defaults in this greatly enlarged loan program? There will be very few. Why?

(3) In this sounder scheme, all students who decide to take the loan will sign a binding agreement with the U.S. government. As soon as they start working after graduation, the money will *automatically* be deducted from their paycheck and sent to the Treasury. Repayment will be at any pace they decide, for a period up to ten years, or even longer.

That will save at least $3 billion a year in defaults, and considerably more in future years as the present program becomes increasingly insolvent.

(4) What about the banks? Right now, they're scalping Uncle Sam by charging him more than the prime rate, a rate that they give to their best customers. (*Nobody* is a better customer than Uncle Sam.) The student pays 8% once he starts to pay it back, but when the market rates are higher, the government pays the bank the difference—a subsidy that has already been above three points.

That should be stopped immediately. Since there is *no risk* for the banks, and they will no longer have to process and approve loans, or collect the money, they should be required to charge no more than the prime. This should save the government about $1 billion a year.

So far, we've saved $6 billion in no-longer-needed Pell Grants, $3 billion in defaults, and another $1 billion or so in interest subsidies, plus more in administrative costs. We've reduced the deficit by at least $10 billion and provided funds for *everyone* to go to college without worry.

Not bad. But most important, we've made a lot of middle-class families, on Long Island and elsewhere, happy.

65

SUBWAYS

It's Free Underground

Is UNCLE SAM in the subway business?

Yes, heavily. The Federal Transit Administration has spent scores of billions thus far to subsidize city subway systems, and not always with the most positive results. Americans continue their love affair with the automobile. But that is another story.

This is the tale of one aspect of one subway—the Washington Metro underground—but it carries a special message for the American taxpayer. Simply stated, it offers a visible example that tax money is considered little more than Monopoly play currency by the federal bureaucracy, who are continually searching for ingenious ways to tap into the overdrawn Treasury.

The Metro was built with the help of $7.7 billion in federal funds (70% of the cost), and the government still subsidizes its operation with $16 million a year for operations and $49 million for capital improvements.

Isn't that enough? Apparently not.

In 1991, a Maryland Senator introduced a bill permitting well-paid federal employees to ride the subway absolutely *free* of charge up to $250 a year worth of fares, which would be paid to the Metro by the rider's government agency. The bill was passed, then signed by the President.

To be sure the taxpayer gift was used, the freebie was even advertised in the subway: "Uncle Sam wants you to ride Metrorail."

The cost? Up to $92 million a year.

This giveaway is a flagrant example of Washington callousness that should not go unnoticed. It suggests that both houses of the U.S. Congress need to curtail the range of their legislation, most of which is an affront to hard-pressed taxpayers.

Perhaps—just perhaps—we need a Constitutional amendment that would require that while the government is in deficit, *all* appropriations have to be approved by 60% of Congress before becoming law. Or maybe self-policing can be a substitute. Congress could pass a resolution requiring that *two* full committees, instead of one, pass judgment, *in public*, on all legislation before it is brought to the floor.

For once, I am stymied—by the subway giveaway. Doesn't anybody in Washington care?

66

SUPERFUND

Slow, Inefficient, and Expensive

EVERYONE HAS HEARD of toxic wastes and the problems they present. Throughout the country, the EPA (Environmental Protection Agency) has identified 1250 sites, from contaminated landfills to old metal plants, from rubber factories to industrial areas with radium-contaminated wastes, that need to be cleaned up. The greatest danger is to the "ground water," the series of underground streams that provide us with much of our drinking water. Mercury, lead, and other poisons lurk unseen.

The EPA began a program in 1980 to get it all cleaned up, and money has been thrown at the subject ever since. Finally tagged "Superfund," it projects the image of an efficient space-borne warrior working on behalf of the environment.

The reality is quite the opposite. The Superfund has been the scene of one of the worst snafus in the history of governmental action—or in this case, inaction and waste.

After $15 billion was appropriated, and now that $10 billion has been spent, the program has been tagged as highly susceptible to "fraud, waste, and abuse."

The first part of the record is expensive sloth. The EPA projects they will add 900 more sites during the 1990s.

How much progress are they making, and how quickly? A report to Congress shows dramatic inaction. By October 1986, only 25 of the sites had been cleaned up. Today, 11 years after the program began, how many of the 1250 are finished? Only 65.

"Considering the time and resources consumed," a GAO official understated to the House Committee on Public Works, "the number of sites cleaned up has been disappointingly small. . . . Sites that have entered the Superfund pipeline have become clogged in a lengthy study and evaluation process, and few have emerged from the end of the pipeline."

Since 95% of the sites are unfinished, at the present pace many will still be uncleaned by the end of the century. The EPA estimates that $40 billion is a minimum figure for the *current* jobs. Up to $125 billion will be needed to handle all sites, including those projected—if the number can be held to 2150, which everyone doubts.

One major cause of the delay is the excessive time it takes to design a cleanup scheme, a problem that is getting worse. Site studies once expected to take two years are now lasting four years or longer. The cleanup plans involve many systems, including incineration and clay "caps" for landfills to keep wastes from escaping. New landfills require a liner base—much like a swimming pool—to keep the hazardous materials from seeping into the soil and groundwater below.

The EPA gets very few gold stars for its work. Waste in handling the hazardous waste is apparently an ongoing failing. The EPA gives out most of its contracts on a cost-reimbursable basis, which can be an invitation to financial disaster. To compound matters, the agency generally permits contractors to estimate the cost of the work without checking up on them. When one contractor estimated the cleanup at a radium plant at $3 million, the EPA did their own independent study. They found it could be done for $1.6 million.

The Superfund people are equally poor at management it seems. Only 30% of the money spent so far has gone for cleanup. One reason administrative charges have been too high is that, in their enthusiasm, EPA "hired more cleanup contractors than it needed," says an audit report.

Another large waste is "indemnification." Though many contractors seem able to secure insurance in non-federal jobs (for causing damage to nearby landowners), they claim it's hard to get it for government work. The result is that the government holds them harmless for damage they may cause, assuming liability for any potential lawsuits.

The contractors submit monthly cost vouchers, which the EPA pays—it turns out—without going over most of them. In one case, a government "floor check" of labor costs billed to the EPA found that less than half the employees involved were actually on the job. In another case, the EPA was billed $180,000 for labor costs that involved 11,000 hours of excess off-time and vacations.

When the GAO looked to see why EPA people weren't auditing the vouchers before they were paid, they were shocked to discover that the staff people "had difficulty reading and understanding the invoices, and lack the guidance and training to do reviews well."

As with the health and science research grants (see RESEARCH, UNIVERSITIES) the EPA also picks up part of the contractor's overhead, which can be an invitation for fancy pencilwork.

In testimony before the House Committee on Energy and Commerce, the Assistant Comptroller General described an audit conducted on a large engineering firm that did work on Superfund sites. They found that the company was charging Uncle Sam for such "indirect" costs as tickets to sporting events, liquor at company parties, travel by employees' spouses, general advertising for "image," and even the loss on the sale of a relocated employee's house.

The audit also turned up $873,000 in "excessive charges for the firm's aircraft." The luxury "unallowables" included $4100 for tickets to the Denver Nuggets, Seattle Mariners, and Seattle Seahawks games, and $7700 for alcoholic beverages.

Generous Uncle Sam even pays for company parties and picnics if they "improve employee morale." The company claimed $19,600 for entertainment, $300 for party invitations, $850 for photographers, $3200 for a dance band, and even $100 for a dance instructor. The audit spokesman pointed out that while the charges weren't being disallowed, he "questioned" whether they were reasonable.

The lessons of the Superfund are many, and they all require rapid attention. They also offer lessons on how to curb other government waste as well:

(1) Cost-plus contracts are foolish, as any homeowner building a house knows. They should be made illegal on all government contracts through explicit legislation in Congress.

(2) The whole question of paying any part of a company's "overhead" rightly makes taxpayers angry. If companies want to drink, party, dance, even fornicate, they can do it on their own dollar. Again, Congress should pass legislation making it illegal for government agencies to pay overhead for anyone at any time. (Wasteful govern-

ment overhead is bad enough.) If there are indirect costs, companies can include them when they bid for a job, which one would hope would be on a competitive basis.

(3) The Superfund is a special case in point. It requires a total management overhaul, a clean sweep, and a new beginning. Spending money on management consultants to fix the disaster called the EPA would probably save us billions as we discover more and more hazardous sites that need cleaning.

The Superfund is "super" in only one way: in the super-billions of taxpayer money being wasted getting rid of the waste.

67

TECHNOLOGY TRANSFER

What Happens to Our R&D?

RESEARCH AND DEVELOPMENT is on everyone's tongue.

Japan and Germany are putting a larger percentage of their GNP into research than we are, preparing to beat America in the international competition of the twenty-first century.

Are we doing anything about it? We say we are, especially at the federal level. In our fight for survival, the government budget for technology and health research rises continually, and according to a recent report, has now reached $17 billion a year for just in-house scientific operations.

The theory is simple. Government science and health researchers are encouraged to develop new discoveries and inventions. Then Washington tries to get them out into the private sector where they can be put to use. Two laws, the Patent and Trademark Amendments of 1980 and the Federal Technology Transfer Act of 1986, were passed to help accomplish this goal of moving America forward in the great technology race, a favorite topic of politicians.

The discoveries are patented in the government's name, and the inventors are given only a small piece of the action: generally 20%, with a yearly cap of $100,000 if the patent clicks in the commercial world, as in the case of the AIDS test developed at the National Institutes of Health.

Overall, how has the licensing of federal patents done in the real world? Poorly, which should surprise no one familiar with the Washington Establishment.

The first part of the program has been successful. That is, the government scientists produced more than 1000 patents in 1991. It was the second part, getting them into the mainstream, that was pitifully unsuccessful.

"We studied the research work done by government scientists and found that the technology transfer from government to industry was *small*," reports an investigator.

The figures support his pessimism. In twelve government agencies, plus sixteen Department of Energy contract labs, the government researchers were busy churning out numerous inventions in the decade of 1980–90. In that period, they received patents for more than 11,000 discoveries that could advance American technology.

Did most of this new knowledge get to industry and the public and put to use?

Not really.

In that same period, only 1400 patents—or 13% of the total—were licensed for private use by the National Institutes of Science and Technology, the National Institutes of Health, and others.

Why?

"A lot of American companies just don't know what patents are available for licensing, and the government is not doing a good job of getting the word out," says the technology auditor. "The universities do a much better job of selling their discoveries than does the federal government. They have specialists doing the work, and it's quite good. I'd say that MIT is probably the best."

The irony is that most of the research work done at the universities is supported by the government. Under federal law, nonprofit organizations doing research with government money can patent and license any discovery that results.

In many cases, the first time that industry hears about a federal invention is when the government advertises in the *Federal Register* that it is ready to grant an exclusive license on the patent. Then some firms come in and try to offer Washington better terms. A General Accounting Office study of the process, which was quite negative, reveals that Uncle Sam "does not effectively get information to company managers who might be interested in the invention."

Some licensing officials offered another reason. The whole process takes too long, typically between one and two *years*, by which time many people give up in frustration.

What is the solution to converting that $17 billion of research effort into useful economic gain?

Here are a few suggestions:

(1) Split 50–50 with the inventors on the royalties instead of offering the present stingy 20%. With that incentive, some scientists may find a way to get the word out. The license income is small and not that important—*if* Washington really wants to transfer technology into the mainstream.

(2) Hire MIT experts to do the selling, or to train Washington how to do it. Federal expertise is in *spending* money, not earning it.

(3) Set up a regular advertising program in such pub-

lications as the *Wall Street Journal* or the *New York Times* to insert short notices of new government patents available for license.

We've got to do something.

Hiding thousands of taxpayer-supported inventions under Washington's bureaucratic hat is one invention we can do without.

68

TRAVEL

Palm Springs or Bust

"WE'VE GOT $49,000 left in our travel budget," a government bureaucrat confided in a travel agency. "Get us some meetings. We'll figure out what they're about later."

This startling quote is taken from the careful research of Congressman Lamar Smith, Republican of Texas.

Smith has been studying government travel expenses, something that is impossible to pin down in the cleverly obfuscated federal budget where there is no such category. (Too easy to check up on.) The figure he has come up with is a startling $7 billion a year, about as much as we spend on Head Start, the National Science Foundation, and school lunches combined.

The Congressional Budget Office adds that in 1991, federal travel costs rose 11.5% in just one year. As one travel supervisor told Smith: "There's plenty of fluff in that budget."

There is no greater perk for a bureaucrat than the exhilarating privilege (though he believes it is a "right") to get out of the office and travel to some distant point on the government's tab—often to a convention meeting or seminar held in a resort area. In fact, during the last month of the fiscal year, as the opening quote indicates, a travel frenzy seizes the federal agencies, which must spend the money or return it to the Treasury.

During that month, there are rush bookings to such popular spots as Las Vegas and Palm Springs, Smith learned.

"We found that supervisors assigned travel dollars to employees to spend before the end of the year," says the hard-nosed Texan. The facts back him up. During the last month of the fiscal year, there was a 48% increase in government travel. He estimates that the taxpayers will lose $1.6 billion just from this last-minute travel stampede.

The whole question of civil servants traveling about the country so freely, and for free, is an issue Congress and the President must address. Judging from other excesses, a conservative guess would be that 50% of it is unnecessary and wasteful.

The solution:

(1) Make year-end travel over the usual allotment illegal.

(2) Re-educate the agency chiefs on how *not* to travel at government expense.

(3) Cut the travel budget from $7 billion to $4 billion, an immediate savings of $3 billion. Then look at the allotment again in a few years to see if it can be reduced further.

The Washington Establishment has been up in the air long enough. It's time to bring them rudely down to earth—but not into Palm Springs.

69

URBAN GARDENS AND THE EXTENSION SERVICE

An Agency for All Reasons

IN THE ERA just before World War I, when America was still basically a rural nation, a visit to the farmhouse from the County Extension Service, a federal-state-local offshoot of the Department of Agriculture, was a welcome one.

It wasn't just a social event, but a chance for the woman of the house to learn, from a professional, the latest techniques in the art of homemaking. Without daily newspapers, or radio and television, the advice from the "home economics" lady was invaluable.

There was instruction, sometimes right alongside the sink and stove, on how to preserve foods, how to can, how to cook certain dishes, how to be sure the food was safe. And the information was up to the moment. Advice on food nutrition, a new science, was freely imparted to the lady of the farm.

At the same time, the County Agricultural Agent of the Extension Service came to see the man of the house. The visitor was a trained specialist, bringing the latest knowledge on planting, seeds, irrigation, hybrid plants, and animal husbandry to the farmer, who was usually uneducated and appreciated learning the new techniques.

The information came directly from the university—one of the Land Grant Colleges established in 1862 during Lincoln's Administration with a view toward educating those in rural areas. Each of the colleges was given aid from the government to start an agricultural school. From there, the knowledge was disseminated to the farms and neighboring community by the Extension Service.

"Bringing the university to the people," was their slogan, and they were justly proud. It was a perfect chain, and the nation gained from it in raising food, settling the frontier, and in strengthening family values. The Extension Service even started the 4H Clubs, one of the more successful youth movements in America. In fact, it might be said that the government of America then—unlike today—was a practical, inexpensive, and effective one.

America has changed dramatically since then. The full-time farming community has shrunk to 1 million farmers, a minuscule portion of the nation. There are few farm housewives waiting for the Home Ec lady to show up, which she seldom does these days anyway. Good nutrition is no longer a university secret now that information is available from magazines, newspapers, radio, and television.

But the handful of farmers left still need the research information brought to them by the ubiquitous County Agent, right? Not necessarily.

"In the old days, the County Agent was full of new knowledge from the university and the farmer was uneducated," says a veteran Department of Agriculture official. "But today, it's often the other way around. Full-time commercial farmers are generally better educated in agriculture than the County Agent, who is likely to be trained in rural sociology or agricultural economics. The regular farmer generally by-passes the County Agent and goes right to the Land Grant agricultural schools, locally, or anywhere in the country."

So if the Extension Service is no longer needed to bring the university to rural areas, hasn't it lost its mission? Is it embarrassedly fading away along with the American farmer?

Not if you know how the U.S. government works. As its mission decreases, the agency thrives by twisting its mandate into ever-new bureaucratic forms.

The Extension Service—in partnership with cooperating states and localities—now employs well over 10,000 people and has offices in almost all of the nation's 3150 counties. Its federal budget alone is $417 million.

What could they possibly do with all that money? And if not on the farm, where?

In the urban and suburban areas, naturally. But what could an agricultural organization do in the city? Leave that to bureaucratic ingenuity.

In Manhattan, about twenty vacant lots tended by local people are flourishing. To beautify the drab environment? No, they are re-creating rural America, growing food with the slight assistance of the Urban Gardening people of the Extension Service, in a $3.5 million national project.

"The program is designed to help them raise their own food so they can have a more nutritious diet," a spokesman says with a straight face. Perhaps 200 citizens are involved in Manhattan, and the gardening staff's main contact with the amateur farmers is a newsletter.

The modern Extension people talk about "family programs," and "financial planning advice," and "consumer education," and "nutrition information" for low-income city people. They employ more than 2500 home-economics specialists, even though house visits, unlike in the prairie days, are rare. They have horticulturists and economists and educators and environmentalists, anything you might want. A duplicating, overlapping, full-service agency—doing what?

Four hundred million dollars is a lot of money. **What should be done with it?**

The obvious answer is to reduce the agency in the same proportions as we have lost farmers—their true clients—since it all began in 1914. That means reducing it by 80%. Retain some agricultural specialists (*not* sociologists) in the heavy farm areas and in the agricultural colleges. Close down the home-economics department, and forget all that loose talk about "family programs." We have dozens of federal agencies already doing a poor job at that.

The savings would be $300 million, which is not cow waste. It would also provide a lesson for Washington in how to sharpen both its missions and its budget pencil.

Besides, who would want to eat broccoli grown in the exhaust of Manhattan buses?

70

VICE PRESIDENT

No Longer Anonymous—or Cheap

VERY FEW AMERICANS can recall the names of more than a half dozen Vice Presidents, if that many. The most famous ones were probably Aaron Burr (under Jefferson), Teddy Roosevelt (under McKinley), and, of course, Harry Truman, the VP of all time, who served under FDR in his fourth term.

Aside from being anonymous, most Vice Presidents had one other endearing quality—they didn't cost much.

Harry was among the cheapest. He had a little office off the Senate floor, with three clerks, and he didn't even have a Secret Service guard when he first took office. He, Bess, and daughter Margaret lived in an apartment house on Connecticut Avenue, where he paid the $140-a-month rent out of his $10,000 salary.

My, how things have changed.

The Vice President now enjoys a near-royal life-style and a staff to fit. He has twenty-six employees (doing what?) and three offices—one in the White House, Harry Truman's old place in the Senate, and a large suite in the Old Executive Office Building. He has more than one limousine, a Secret Service driver, in addition to an around-the-clock protection squad, and access to a giant Boeing 707, which automatically becomes Air Force Two when he boards it.

No two-bedroom apartment for him. The Vice President lives in a large government-supported Victorian mansion on the grounds of the Naval Observatory in the District, which first became the Veep's home under Walter Mondale in 1977. In addition to a housekeeper, who earns $50,000 a year, the Vice President has a crew of Navy men (on the Defense Department tab) who take care of his grounds. His salary is $160,600 a year, and he receives a $90,000 entertainment allowance to use as he sees fit.

Times have sure changed for America's Veeps. All this costs some $5 million a year, which is not the cause of the national debt. But it's a solid symptom.

Harry Truman, where are you when we need you?

71

WATER SUBSIDIES

Wet Behind the Ears

"WHEN PEOPLE THINK of farms, they conjure up images of the Little House on the Prairie," says a government attorney. "Well, the big farms in Imperial Valley and central California—once arid land made fertile with government irrigation water—are nothing like that.

"Some are giant operations, as large as 15,000 acres and more," he continued. "The owner probably has an airplane, his own airstrip, a recreation hall, barracks for the workers, and a main headquarters in a fancy office building in downtown Los Angeles. Someone once called it 'the Cadillac desert,' which is true. And the taxpayers are helping to pay for it."

Water is king in the great semi-arid Western states. The people, the farms, and the environment all compete for the water that falls from the Rockies and other mountain ranges into the Colorado, the Missouri, the Columbia, and the Sacramento Rivers, then gets dammed up in the colossi of concrete built by the federal government at enormous cost.

From these dams, the water flows not only to towns and cities, but to farmers whose once near-desert land now raises the fruits and vegetables that feed America.

No one wants to deny them the water. Without it, our

Western year-round agriculture would virtually vanish. But instead of paying their fair share, the farmers, including our Imperial Valley millionaire, have—quite legally—stuck the American taxpayers with the bill for an expensive, wasteful, wet federal boondoogle.

The vehicle is "subsidized water," for which farmers pay the government as little as $2 an acre-foot (a foot of water covering an acre of land), when the "true cost," as the Bureau of Reclamation calls it, can run as high as $70. The difference, which some estimate at $1 billion a year, is what we pay in extra taxes.

Why did we let it happen?

Initially, subsidized water was a lure to get people out to settle the West. But after the farms became big business, the government finally realized they had been taken. In 1982, they tried to clamp down on large farms through the Reclamation Reform Act, which limited the amount of land that could receive subsidized water to 960 acres. If a farmer's spread was larger than that—as some in south and central California and Oregon and Washington were—he'd have to pay the full water price on any acreage over 960. Seemed fair enough.

But once again, everyone under-estimated Washington's propensity for irrationality. In this case, the government proved to be ignorant even of its own laws.

Determined to stay on the federal dole, the Western farms split up their large tracts of land into separate 960 acre units, using different corporations, trusts, partnerships, and other interlocking holdings—what a government spokesman calls "paper transactions." Through this loophole, they didn't lose a drop of subsidized water.

"Congressional expectations have not been met," says a General Accounting Office report. "The Reclamation Reform Act . . . does not preclude multiple landholdings

. . . to continue to be operated collectively as one large farm while individually qualifying for federally subsidized water."

Checking on just one farm with 23,000 acres, the GAO found that the land had been sold to 326 trust beneficiaries, and was legally eligible to receive the full subsidy, which cost the government $2 million in lost water revenues. Says a discouraged official: "We recommended to Congress that they change the law to make the 960-acre limit stick, but nothing has happened."

So the next time you buy a high-priced cantaloupe from California's Imperial Valley in the cold of winter, just remember that you're paying twice.

Once for the melon, and again for the taxpayer's mountain water that made it grow.

72

WHITE HOUSE STAFF

The President's Men

THE WHITE HOUSE was once a lean operation with relatively few people around the President.

Before World War II, FDR managed with fewer than 200 on his staff, excluding the people handling the budget. In the burgeoning postwar world, Harry Truman did fine with only 285 people. Even Jack Kennedy, with his broad aspirations, was able to hold the White House organization down to 375.

But since then, the operation at 1600 Pennsylvania Avenue has mirrored the growth in big government.

Today, the White House has 1850 employees (1250 excluding the budget people), which is more than three times as many as under JFK. The President's total White House budget is $300 million, and the mansion itself is the least of the cost, with fewer than 100 employees (even with four in-house florists) and a budget of $11 million.

It's the enormous staff that works out of the Executive West Wing, the Old Executive Office Building across the street, and the nearby New Executive Office Building that eats up the dollars. These people are not cheap to come by, with several in the six-figure salary range, and others not far behind.

Why do Presidents now need so many people when Chief Executives used to make do with less?

Critics believe that the basic reason—along with the general laxity of management discipline in government—is that contemporary Presidents want to keep as much power as possible under their own hats in the White House. They prefer not to have to rely on their Cabinet members, who run the federal agencies with quite a bit of independence. In a way, the White House staff is competing with the Cabinet members in a contest for power, and in doing so, duplicates the work of many federal agencies.

Presidents don't seem to mind the waste. It means they have their own people close at hand who specialize in such areas as drugs, environment, national security, technology, economics, trade, space—subjects on which fortunes are being spent in the regular federal agencies.

Does the President need such a large staff? No. Not if the expensive Cabinet system set up by the Constitution is to mean anything.

The solution?

Simple. Cut the White House organization down to a manageable 600 (excluding the budget people, who'll be needed to do it), which is still almost double Kennedy's entourage.

The saving will be in the range of $100 million or so.

It's not peanuts, but most important, the President will be speaking from his "bully pulpit" in showing other Washington administrators that the deficit can really be beaten.

And besides, he can then take credit for fighting "big government."

73

WOOL AND MOHAIR

Shearing the Taxpayer

As WE'VE SEEN, when Washington gets an idea, it starts a program that goes on and on—even if the original premise has long since disappeared.

This is the case with the wool project of the Department of Agriculture, which began in the 1950s when the Defense Department feared they wouldn't have enough wool for uniforms and coats, especially in areas with cold climates.

They set to work with the farm lobby and sheep raisers to increase American production so that GI Joe would never freeze in the Alaskan—or even Siberian—wastes. And once again, Uncle Sam put up bushels of money to achieve the goal.

How has it all worked out?

Well, to give away the punch line, the results have been nothing short of catastrophic. The need is gone but the fiscal injury lingers on. As the General Accounting Office reports: "Overall, wool production has *declined* substantially since the wool-payment program began."

In 1955, when the Pentagon declared wool a "strategic" item that needed stockpiling, Congress passed the National Wool Act to ensure continued production at prices fair to producers and consumers. At the time, the industry was healthy. Wool production was 282 million pounds.

But today, 37 years later, after the government has invested $2 billion in subsidies for sheep farmers, production has dropped precipitously to 89 million pounds, a clear bottom point.

What happened?

First, the plan was not well thought out. Even though the subsidies were outrageously high, it cost the government more than the market price to lift production even a bit, gains that were finally illusory. The General Accounting Office reports that in 1988, any additional output cost the government $3.04 a pound when the market price was only $1.38.

At that point the reason for the whole program had evaporated anyway. In 1960, just five years after it began, the Defense Department reevaluated its "strategic" material needs. They decided that wool was not needed after all. They used only 8% of the domestic production, which would always be available, and synthetic fibers were replacing wool in cold-climate clothing.

The Pentagon was no longer involved, but the farm lobby was firmly entrenched. The subsidies kept rolling along, and are in place today exactly as they were in 1955. Not only do sheep farms still receive federal money for their wool, but the government also pays a subsidy for "unshorn" lambs, a logic that defies explanation. One reason the subsidies have had little effect is that sheep farmers get 75% of their income from selling lambs for meat, not for their wool.

In 1991, the government spent almost $100 million futilely trying to lift wool production, even if no one remembers why. Meanwhile, another commodity, mohair—the hair of Angora goats—has not only sneaked into the subsidy program, but has become the major taker of Uncle Sam's wool money.

What can be done?

This solution is as easy as counting sheep. Cut out the outdated project, and pocket the $100 million to reduce the deficit. Wool production in the U.S. will stay just where it is—at its low point in history—with or without the taxpayers' cash.

"The whole program has been a disaster," says a government agricultural specialist. "It's time to shut it down."

74

YOUTH

Let's Start Over Again

"WE'RE DOING a pilot program in several cities," said a spokesman for YOU, Youth Opportunity Unlimited, a young people's program sponsored by the Department of Labor. "We're putting money into a Boys' and Girls' Club in San Diego, for example, and adding staff to see if we can help out. Our program offers sports, outings, and recreation for under-privileged youth. The whole program costs $25 million over a period of years and it'll be a while before it's fully under way."

This sounds strangely like a successful old concept of the private sector's that has been around for over a century in such institutions as the YMCA and YWCA, the YMHA, the Play Schools Association, the Boys' and Girls' Clubs, and the Settlement Houses, which were well established in such immigrant areas as the Lower East Side of New York long before the social work profession ever came into being.

Unfortunately, the idea had been lost, or misplaced, by the American government. A study of what Washington offers teenagers today turns up a short list that concentrates on the *negative* aspects of our society. Health and Human Services gives money for Runaway Youths. The National Institute for Drug Abuse tries to help addicted teenagers. The Public Health Service has a program for pregnant teenage girls. And so on.

These are worthwhile projects, but what is seriously missing from the federal agenda are *positive* activities for teenagers. A search of the budget turns up only three programs, with a total allotment of about $20 million a year. With that relatively small sum, a handful of government people—perhaps without realizing it—are trying to do something old-fashioned: to provide a healthy environment of diversion, sports, entertainment, and recreation for a restless generation.

The YOU program is seeking to develop and expand youth community centers in a number of cities. The Youth-at-Risk project of the Department of Agriculture (though a little off the farm path) is spending part of its $7.5 million budget to start after-school programs. In the sports area, the NCAA spends $9 million of government money for a summer program for youngsters ten to sixteen years old who can play everything from badminton to tennis on college campuses across the country.

The teen problem is not just one for the inner cities. Greenwich, Connecticut, one of the nation's most affluent towns, has its own youth problem. It is starting to attack it with a teen community center, which has had a successful beginning.

The government is slowly rediscovering the old concept that providing a wholesome recreational environment for youngsters, with concentration on moral values integrated with a curriculum of fun, can bear good future gains. But in typical Washington fashion, the three youth programs are run by three different agencies—Labor, Agriculture, and Health and Human Services. They should be united under one umbrella and perhaps tried out on a larger scale: reinforcing and creating community centers across America for young people and teenagers, where the *positive* aspects of life in our country can be stressed in a warm, non-social-work, recreational environment.

Well, you say, that costs money. Yes, but we've saved so many billions thus far in this book, perhaps we can be excused for investing perhaps $100 million to roll back the clock for our youth. It's better than gangs, drugs, and teenage pregnancy.

Who knows, maybe in the long run it'll even save us some money.

75

ZOOS

The Pandas Live in One

THE UNITED STATES OPERATES two in Washington, D.C.

One is called the National Zoological Park, and it is a 163-acre parcel between Rock Creek Park and Connecticut Avenue in the mainly residential northwest area of the city.

Founded in 1889, the park gets 3 million visitors a year, has 300 federal employees, and is best known as the home of the Chinese panda bear couple, who have tried unsuccessfully to produce a surviving cub.

The park has a federal budget of $16 million, and is in the midst of an $8 million renovation. This new spending is consistent with its parent, the giant Smithsonian Institution, surely the most costly and extravagant museum organization in the world, or in the history of the world.

The Smithsonian employs 4767 people, and has requested a budget of $331 million for 1993, a rise of over $100 million just since 1990. It is a prime example of how our government enthusiastically expands on borrowed money in an unsure economy.

The second zoo? It is the mother of them all. To get there, you walk one block from the National Zoo and get on the Red Line at the Woodley Park Metro station. You go two stops to the Farragut North station and walk three blocks south.

From there, you walk two more blocks to the Farragut West station and take the Blue Line to Federal Center Southwest. From there it is just four blocks north.

In that short excursion, you've reached both the White House and the Capitol building, the Pennsylvania Avenue power axis of Washington's second zoo—the federal government of the United States.

With, of course, our apologies to the charming pandas.

CONCLUSION

How to Reform the
United States Government

THE GOVERNMENT IN WASHINGTON is out of control—
fiscally, morally, and philosophically.

It wastes a great deal of money, as we have seen, but
the problem is even broader and deeper. The federal
government no longer has a clear concept of how it's
supposed to operate, and has become a victim of its own
expansion.

The country envisioned by Jefferson and Madison had
built-in restraints. If an issue was parochial in nature, it
was left to the States. The federal apparatus was reserved
for grander issues, such as war and peace and the general
welfare.

The Tenth Amendment to the Constitution, the last
item in the Bill of Rights, was supposed to guarantee that
separation of powers between Washington and the States.
But that clause is not enforced. Instead it is virtually
swept aside in the rush of overwhelming national problems and would-be solutions.

In prior chapters, we've seen examples of our government's outrageous inefficiency, along with this author's
suggestion for cuts. These, along with a gradual reduction
in defense outlays will go a long way toward bringing the

budget under control. But that can only happen *if* the government begins a sensible retrenchment.

Can real change take place under the present Washington structure? Is the federal government set up to carry out a reform that will bring it soundly into the twenty-first century?

Absolutely not.

Simply stated, our government is presently too big and too unresponsive to make a 180-degree change. The federal apparatus served us well until a quarter century ago, but it no longer functions the way it was designed. The pressures of heightened expectations; an active media, especially television; raucous election campaigns; race relations; political financing; poverty; sophisticated special interests lobbying for themselves—plus the philosophical and moral failure of many politicians—have made the present way of handling our government business outdated, even impractical.

The framework of freedom is there, and must be maintained at all costs. But the daily routine of our democratic operations, from the Congress to the Presidency, has locked us into a pattern of failure. If we are to break out, we must restructure the federal government.

Here then, is a plan.

Of the three branches of government, the Judiciary is the least expensive, and the only one that has survived the test of time. The other two branches—the Legislative and Executive—have strayed far from the design envisioned by the Founding Fathers.

To lay out a blueprint for change, we will concentrate on those two, offering a scheme in four parts: the Congress; the Presidency and the Executive Branch; the Budget, which involves both branches; and last, Election Campaign Reform.

CONGRESS

The House of Representatives and the Senate, established in 1789 as a compromise between the small and the populous states, continue under fire, with heads bent. But despite their liabilities, they are still the core of our democracy. If our nation is to stay great, the Congress must be rescued *from itself.*

What has gone wrong?

Almost everything. But let's start with an important failing:

Congressional Committees

Since the days of the "great reform" in the 1970s when the Young Turks threw out the old dictatorial seniority system, anarchy has reigned on the Hill. The number of committees—standing, joint, select—and subcommittees has reached almost 300, creating a somewhat mad spectacle, leaving little time for contemplation.

More than half our Congressmen are now Committee Chairmen, which elevates their egos and fills their calendars. The hearings go on without end, keeping the Government Printing Office busy turning out testimony records, most of which languish and serve no one.

Politicians have always been ambitious egoists, but the army of Chairmen on the Hill exaggerates that failing. With both eyes on the media, they hope their chairmanships will bring them the brass ring—fame, repeated reelection, a Senate seat if they are Representatives, power, and perhaps even a shot at the Presidency. The Congress has become a coliseum of over-ambitious men and women.

The committee system is a necessary part of Congress and should not be abolished. But the number of committees must be cut drastically—at least in half. This will reduce the number of chairmen, returning 150 Congressmen to the ranks, where they belong—working for the people.

The same is true of committee staffs, an army of professionals who overwhelm everyone, including Congressmen themselves. There are now 3700 staff members— five times more than in Kennedy's time—helping to make Washington ever more complex and unwieldy.

The committee staff should be cut in half as well, to under 2000. Perhaps that would let a little light, and space, into the over-crowded, over-busy halls of Congress.

Personal Staffs

In the days of FDR, the Congress passed an enormous amount of legislation, yet it was accomplished with personal staffs of *only two people* for each member of the House. Even in the more complex postwar days of Harry Truman, Congressmen had only five staffers.

Today, the 535 members of both houses of Congress employ almost 12,000 personal staff people, an impossible army that must be thinned out. (Remember, each House member has 18 full-timers and a few part-timers, while Senators have 40 staffers each.) Congressmen devote too much time to managing, which has nothing to do with their job of representing the voters.

There is no magical formula, but for now, we'll stick to the simple equation of cutting things in half. By reducing the personal staff to 6000, there will be more room, not only to move, but to think. And if there's anything lacking in the halls of Congress, it's that simple exercise.

Leaders

Congress is leadership-happy, especially in the House. They have six in addition to the Speaker: the Majority Leader, the Minority Leader, the Whips of both parties, and the Chief Deputy Whips. With their combined staff of almost 150, they ride herd on their fellow Congressmen, trying to bend them to the party line. They receive extra salary, spacious offices, staff and perks, and have generally been successful in making Congress a mechanical body that follows orders.

The two-party system in Congress is not only solidified, it's ossified. If Congressmen decide on an independent stand, they're not showing courage, according to the leaders. They're traitors. The vote on the Gulf War was a case in point: the vote came down heavily on party lines, as it does on most issues. By and large, the people in both chambers do not vote their consciences, but follow the orders of the Congressional leaders.

There's an old adage in Congress: "to get along, go along." It's not just a cliché, it's unwritten law. Most Congressmen know that if they don't follow party orders, there's little chance for promotion or chairmanships. They might even be inviting a primary fight back home.

What can be done to stimulate independent, idiosyncratic opinion in our representatives?

The only way is to weaken the power of the leadership. Though they masquerade as Congressional officers, and are paid extra salaries out of the Treasury, they actually perform party functions. Nowhere in the Constitution does it mention political parties, and the citizens—many of whom are independents—should not be taxed to support them.

What should be done? Let the leaders retain their

titles, if they want, but all of their staffs, offices, and special perks should be eliminated. The same is true of the government-paid salaries and expenses of the Democratic Caucus and the Republican Conference in Congress.

(Incidentally, the party leaders are the last ones in the House to receive large perks. All the free cars should be taken away from Congressmen, and the leadership stripped of their Capitol police-chauffeurs and their salary bonuses. Democracy is nourished best on humble pie.)

These moves are not just to save money, but to break the party stranglehold—whether Democratic or Republican—on Congress, something that has contributed to the body's gridlock.

With the exception of the Speaker of the House, who is elected by all members, the American people can do without "official" leaders in Congress. And surprisingly enough, so can the Congressmen.

Lobbyists

They represent a creeping disease that threatens the nation.

There are more than 6000 lobbyists registered with the Clerk of the House, and they represent every special-interest group in the nation—except the people.

It would be different if these people were as ineffective as our elected officials and bureaucrats. But they are not. They are smart, well financed, and very effective. In fact, few laws are passed in our august legislature that don't bear the direct imprint of some lobbyist.

What can be done?

First, we should bar former Congressmen from lobbying their ex-colleagues for a period of five years. No one is as effective as a buddy who once sat beside you, and who is now making twice as much money as you are. Former Representatives can walk right into the Cloakroom and *onto* the floor of the House and, in the case of Senators, onto both floors. Those practices should be discontinued immediately.

Additionally, it should be illegal for Congressmen to accept any entertainment—drinks, lunch, breakfast, dinner, et cetera—from any lobbyists. Since few Congressmen would pick up a tab, that should slow down the warm lobbyist-to-legislator contact that now costs us so much money, and creates such potential for harm.

Financial limits should also be placed on registered lobbyists. Some lobby organizations spend millions influencing Congress. A strict cap should be placed on those expenditures.

These moves can and will help. But no matter what we do, lobbyists, like death and taxes, will always be with us. Our Congressmen need to realize that, no matter how much they agree with a lobbyist's stand, or like him personally, they are the *adversaries*, and not the friends, of the people.

If we're ever to have a government not dominated by special interests, as this one is, it will require a better philosophical understanding of what makes decent politics on the part of our legislators.

Pork

Pork barrel appropriations are among the most debilitating aspects of the U.S. Congress.

As we've seen, they're often ludicrous and expensive,

as in the study of the sex life of the quail or the building of a giant replica of the Great Pyramid.

But the most damaging aspect of pork is that it's symbolic of much that is wrong in Congress—a kind of pervasive, petty greediness for reelection that violates the nation's true needs.

Most of the pork-barrel waste starts on committees. Because Congress is so busy (even if unproductive), committees have enormous power in setting up bills exactly as they like. That includes inserting little gifts for the folks at home—a university building, a road, a bridge, a grant, a gymnasium, or whatever—into the legislation.

How can we stop it cold?

It won't be easy, but here goes:

The first change should be a Congressional rule that no member of a committee can put pork that benefits his constituency into a bill. That would apply collectively as well. On a bill a committee is considering, no pork would be allowed that singled out *any* of the members' districts for special benefit.

Of course, there's always the chance for political horse trading: "You put me in your bill and I'll put you in mine." But the House can define that as unethical behavior. To give the rule teeth, they should increase the staff of the House Committee on Standards of Official Conduct (the House Ethics Committee) from its present eleven up to twenty. This costs money, but here we're talking peanuts while eliminating pork would save us billions each year.

Another aspect of pork confuses many citizens, including me. Why is it legal and ethical for tax money to be given away—as pork grants now do—to private institutions, such as universities or the YMCA, even though no federal function is involved?

As caring citizens, we may choose to contribute to charities, but there's no good reason for our tax money to be directed there. These grants should be eliminated as well.

Like the lobbyists, pork may stay with us in some form, but we should still fight it as a cancer eating away at our democracy.

THE PRESIDENT AND THE EXECUTIVE BRANCH

I think we've made it clear—no one is really in charge of the government.

This has always been somewhat true because of the checks and balances of the Constitution. But it's gotten worse since the 1960s. If the government is ever to be brought back into control, several changes have to be made.

The first order of business is to bring it down to size. We must drastically reduce the number of federal employees. From the 2.1 million non-postal people on the payroll today, we need to cut 25%. That will bring the federal employee roster down to 1.6 million. Not only will it save almost $100 billion in salaries, benefits, and overhead, it may make it possible for someone to truly run the nation.

The present structure of the Executive Branch is not working. The President's powers are restricted by Congress, which is necessary to protect the people against tyranny. But that only exaggerates the sense of an Executive Branch—whether under Republicans or Democrats—that is rudderless.

No corporation could be run under the present Washington system, in which everything is predicated on politics and almost nothing on efficiency.

What is glaringly missing are two top executives, appointed by the President, who would actually *run* the government day to day in his name: a Chief Operating Officer and a Chief Financial Officer, each with his own staff and the President-given power to cut across all sacrosanct department and agency borders.

But isn't the President's Chief of Staff already his operating officer?

Absolutely not. The Chief of Staff may be the President's Friend and Loyal Counselor, Hatchet Man, and Protector of the President's Back, but he's surely not the operating officer of the government. Neither can the President—with his political, ceremonial, and leadership roles, and daily pressure to react to emergencies (real and imagined)—do that job. Or even truly understand it, no matter how intelligent he is.

Do we need another top executive when we already have Cabinet officers?

Yes, because unfortunately they are part of the problem. Each Cabinet officer is a semi-autonomous ruler who defends his or her fiefdom and budget with great zeal, seeking ever-larger responsibilities, projects, staffs, and accoutrements of power, and the divine right to spend more and more of our money. When Congress doesn't hand over new programs, these officers seek to invent them.

It is the present Cabinet system that has created the enormous overlap and duplication in Washington. Dozens of agencies are simultaneously involved in job training, Indian affairs, loans and grants, education, health, and almost any area you can mention. These departments are proud, rich, and virtually autonomous.

They mainly touch base with the White House when they need more money from Congress in the upcoming budget.

Aside from the Cabinet, doesn't the President already have hundreds of specialists in the West Wing to advise him?

Yes, but they are policy people and not "line" men, and their very pores are political, not executive. A true Chief of Operations would be indifferent to partisan politics, would answer only to the President and the demands of efficiency, and would ride herd on the sloppy, bloated government.

The second missing person in the Executive Branch is a Chief Financial Officer, a key person in any corporation.

True, the President has a director of the Office of Management and Budget. But the new financial officer will serve a different function. He will not be concerned about a politically savvy budget, nor will he yield to Cabinet pressure as does the OMB. Nor will he be defensive about where the money's being spent, as we've seen the OMB do.

Nor will he be secretive about how it's being spent— down to the last penny—whether it's for entertainment, travel, planes and cars, chauffeurs, liquor, defaulted loans, or $7000 for bed sheets.

Together, the two new Chiefs could invade the territory of Cabinet officers and slash away at the overlap and duplication, bringing the same functions under the same roof, with savings in the billions of dollars.

Together, they would not hide—as does the OMB— the embarrassing questions of overhead. Instead, they would reveal it in infinite detail, then start to slash it, ruthlessly, just as would a beleaguered financial officer at GM. They might even finally unravel the great mystery of

"OTHER SERVICES," a budget item that eats up $170 billion of our money each year.

Won't the Cabinet officers scream? Probably, but a well-prepared President committed to change would already have their signed resignations waiting in his bottom desk drawer.

The first move of the new regime should be to cut the White House staff, a great symbolic gesture to impress the voters.

You may recall that Harry Truman made do with fewer than 300 people (aside from the budget staff), and JFK with fewer than 400, while the White House today has 1250 staffers. Cutting that number in half (Gross's general rule of governmental efficiency) would offer an example in rectitude to the Cabinet people, challenging them to follow suit.

In all this, there's one other executive activity that's urgently needed. That is the Line Item Veto. If it ever becomes a reality, it will put the President on the same power level as 43 of our Governors. It may not be a miracle worker, but it will place Congress on notice that someone with a sharp-pointed pen is watching, poised to strike.

Another change that must be made is in "oversight" of our money. Right now, the General Accounting Office does a creditable job of watching the Executive Branch and turning out hundreds of reports on how money can be saved. Some of its suggestions are taken, but by and large they are ignored by both the Congress and the President. Besides, the competent GAO is part of the Legislative Branch, and they are not permitted to check up on Congress.

In the Executive Branch itself, there are Inspectors General in each department. Some of these also do an excellent job, but what they uncover are individual case histories of fraud and misuse of funds. If they were taken seriously by their agencies—which they generally aren't—their investigations could be seen as *patterns* of excess that could be fixed. But that seldom happens.

What is needed is an independent National Inspector General's Office, which would probe—in addition to the present IGs and the GAO—into everybody's business. Not only would they find fraud, but they would seek out waste as well, and then prepare a semi-annual report to the nation on what they've found and where they've found it—whether in the White House, the bureaucracy, or in Congress.

That team of Chief Operating Officer, Chief Financial Officer, and a National Inspector General could—with the cooperation of the President and the Congress—truly start to turn the nation around.

THE BUDGET: A JOINT RESPONSIBILITY

The great mistake in running America is made at the beginning of each year when we start the budget process.

That is when all the greed and ignorance of Washington rushes to the fore as everyone tries to protect his turf—at the expense of the people of the United States.

This giant error is that we always start with the previous year's budget. It's like spending $20,000 repairing a car that's been totaled in a crash. That prior budget is the result of thousands of errors accumulated over the years, a prime example of fiscal blindness and ineffective operations. Yet we select it as our model, then add insult to injury by allocating still more useless billions each October.

That has to stop.

An intelligent budget process can start in one of two ways.

Option 1: ZBB—Zero-Based Budgeting—in which we try to invent a healthy, sound government from scratch, studying each department and what it needs to perform its job intelligently and economically, and then arrive at a total.

Option 2: the more practical way, set a budget goal—say, $400 billion lower than the present one—and start to make *cuts* in the old budget to fit the *essential* services and the fiscal goal at the same time. Here is where the new Chief Financial Officer and the National Inspector General will shine.

Having done that—while reading the riot act to the Cabinet people as we go—the budget should be solidified at the White House. It should then be brought to the Congress for private, advance discussions.

If the White House comes in with a deficit-free budget, but Congress balks, then the President should race to the television studio. He should tell the people, in infinite detail, how his economic plan is being sabotaged.

But first, of course, he must have one. Most Presidents carp that Congress spends too much money, but Congress responds that no modern President, save only Nixon in one year of his administration, has ever brought a balanced budget to Congress.

And this new budget, unlike the present ones, will be clear and not a masterpiece of obfuscation. All items of overhead—such as travel, computer costs, entertainment, telephone, consultants, furniture, moving, to mention a few—will be listed specifically.

Unlike the current 2000-page budget, the totals for all expenditures, including salaries and benefits for the entire government, will be tallied separately, right up front.

In the present book, you could spend a week with a calculator trying to learn what's going on, but the truth would still elude you.

The government's motive in how the budget is now presented is to confuse the American people. That has to stop.

The next move, which is finally being seriously considered in Congress, is to press for a Balanced Budget Amendment to the Constitution. Most states in the union have it and it works.

Why would it work in Washington? Because if the President and the Congress wanted to spend more than we take in, they would be forced to raise taxes considerably, which would rapidly end their political careers. Right now, the deficit and debt are their convenient avenues of escape.

The only caveat to such a Constitutional amendment is to allow loopholes for extreme emergencies such as war. (We could never have financed World War II out of current income.) And there should be a six-month leeway clause that allows us to balance the books shortly after the fiscal year if we make a financial miscalculation or two.

Gramm-Rudman has failed, as have all other promises to hold the line. Now the people must speak.

ELECTION CAMPAIGN REFORM

If ever a system needed changing it is the way we elect our Presidents, Senators, and Congressmen.

It is now a big-money game, which by definition, excludes most people from the race. Perhaps among our populace there are thousands who would make better Congressmen, even Presidents, than the present contenders. But we will never know because the process requires money—too much money—which is raised with great pain and compromise.

The election process has been destroyed because of the enormous amounts we permit candidates to raise and spend in federal races.

As the system now stands, we, the taxpayers, give each of the Presidential nominees a check for $55 million to run their campaigns once they've been selected by the conventions. We even pay the $11 million tab for each party convention. We not only permit giant, costly, television-commercial-crazed political campaigns, we encourage and pay for them.

The costs connected with running for office make the race painful and the job hollow. If a candidate is continually raising money for his election, as Representatives must, what good is the office or the Congressman's service to the people?

This year, the federal government, through tax form contributions, will give $200 million to support the Presidential election circus. The same money, if used judiciously, could pay for *all* federal elections—House, Senate, and Presidential—without anyone having to raise a copper cent.

How?

Simply by passing three pieces of legislation.

The first would make all political radio and television advertising *illegal*, just as we've done with cigarettes and liquor. That's where much of the money now goes. It will immediately reduce the cost of campaigns and eliminate the corrupt political commercials we're now forced to endure. Instead, the FCC will require television stations to provide free time for candidates.

Second, a ceiling should be put on the cost of all campaigns. In electing a President, including primaries and the general election, that total should be $50 million divided among all candidates.

As for Senators, there should be a total budget of $1 million divided among all candidates for each Senate seat, including incumbents. For each slot in the House, it should be $200,000 for all candidates. These budgets are now exceeded tenfold, and more, by PAC money and other contributions.

Speaking of PAC money, the third piece of legislation is the most important one. It's time to banish almost all private money from the American political system. All PACs would be dissolved.

Except for $250 maximum contributions to their primary campaigns, *no candidate would be allowed to raise any funds, because political contributions for those seeking any federal office would be outlawed.* Similarly, $500—not $20,000—would be the maximum allowable contribution to a political party.

Who then will pay for the campaigns?

In the 1992 Presidential election year, the federal government will spend $200 million of public funds on the campaign. In the new system, it will pay $50 million for the Presidential election, $33 million for the Senate elections (one-third of the seats are generally up), and $86 million for the 435 Congressional races. This totals $169 million in the presidential year, a savings of $31 million.

But more important, anyone who qualifies to get on the ballot will have a modest sum with which to run. It could change the face of American politics by stimulating ordinary citizens to run for office. It will broaden the base of candidates by replacing today's rich cats and ambitious lawyers with teachers, small-business owners, homemakers, blue-collar workers, professors, accountants, all of whom we need in Washington.

This new system will also clear the air of the pollution of political television commercials. It will end the horror of raising money and being beholden to wealthy supporters instead of to the American people.

The plan is radical, but it has a good chance to clean up American campaign politics in one burst of decent enthusiasm. Candidates will have to resort to the soapbox, the whistle stop, public speeches, television talk shows and debates, and face-to-face engagements with the voters if they want to win.

And this new plan needs one last piece of legislation to make it whole.

That is, once we invite average citizens to participate in politics, we have to be ready to kick them out after they've served their time in Washington.

Term limitations are essential. Two terms for Senators, as we now have for Presidents, are sufficient—a total of twelve years. For Representatives, who are closer to the people, four terms of two years each are enough.

The American citizen's frustration with government is not imagined, or without basis. Virtually everything Washington does lacks both intellect and practicality. It's time for the American citizen to become involved, to make Washington once again a place of which we can all be proud.

ABOUT THE AUTHOR

The Government Racket, a critique of waste and inefficiency in Washington, is the fourth nonfiction work of
author, editor, and educator Martin L. Gross.

The former editor of *Book Digest* magazine, Mr. Gross
is an experienced reporter who covered Washington for
many years for national publications and his syndicated
column "The Social Critic," which appeared in such
newspapers as the *Los Angeles Times*, *Newsday*, and the
Chicago Sun-Times. His articles have been published in a
variety of magazines, from *Life* to *The New Republic*.

The author's prior nonfiction works were selections of
major book clubs and aroused significant controversy.

His first, *The Brain Watchers*, a critique of psychological testing, was praised by C. Northcote Parkinson as "a
book that could hardly be bettered." Mr. Gross, called
the "bunkraker" by *Time* magazine, was a leading witness
at Congressional hearings on the subject, resulting in
legislation curtailing their use in federal employment.

His second work, *The Doctors*, an indictment of poor
medical care, received strong support from academic
physicians, including the director of the prestigious Massachusetts General Hospital. The author was attacked by
the AMA, whose organization has since followed most of
his recommendations to improve the quality of medicine
in America.

The author's third work, *The Psychological Society*, was a critique of American psychiatry, setting off a strong controversy within the field. Mr. Gross was the leading witness at a U.S. Senate hearing, which resulted in legislation that followed the author's recommendations for increased research into the causes of mental illness.

His current work, *The Government Racket*, is the result of extensive research on the federal government, including the study of scores of government departments and agencies.

Mr. Gross served on the faculty of the New School for Social Research for many years and is Adjunct Associate Professor of Social Science at New York University.